Silkie Chickens

by

Harry Goldcroft

First Printing, 2013

ISBN 978-0-9926048-0-6

PIB Publishing
13 Pencross View
Hemyock
Cullompton
Devon. EX15 3XH
United Kingdom

Dedication

This book is dedicated to all those that keep and care for these wonderful, fluffy feathered friends. To those who gain enjoyment from having these amazing animals in their lives.

Table of Contents

Chapter 1. Introduction

If there is one type of chicken that I love to talk about, it is the Silkie. Also known as a Silky, this breed of chicken is known for its wonderful appearance and its wonderful temperament.

Playful, affectionate and entertaining are often three words that describe the beautiful Silkie. In addition, these chickens are an interesting breed that can be amazing pets for your backyard.

If you are interested in learning everything you can about the Silkie and owning your own, then you have found the right book. This book looks at the history of the Silkie and goes over some general facts about the breed.

In addition, this book explores how to properly care for your Silkie and also the many different illnesses that can affect them. By the time you are finished reading this book, you will understand everything you need to know about this beautiful, ornamental chicken.

Chapter 2. Getting to know the Silkie

Before we look at raising and breeding Silkies, it is important to get to know the bird on its own. If you are wondering what the Silkie is, it is actually a chicken that is known for its interesting plumage, sweet temper and its reputation as a brooder.

While that snapshot gives you an excellent insight into the Silkie chicken, it doesn't really give you as much information as you would need. In this chapter, I will take you through getting to know the Silkie from what they are to their history. I will also cover general facts about the Silkie, which will get you started in the world of Silkies and show chickens.

1. What is the Silkie?

Also known as Silky, or Silkie Chickens, the Silkie is a breed of chicken that is identified by its soft, down like feathers that give the chicken a silky feel to its feather. They often resemble puffballs, with a fur like feather, and there are actually three different varieties of Silkie chickens; the bearded, non bearded and bantam.

They are characterized by their docile nature that makes them a wonderful pet and backyard chicken. They are usually tamed very easily and are friendly to everyone, including children.

The Silkie chicken is an ornamental chicken and while they do lay, they do not lay as frequently or as many eggs as other breeds. In fact, the Silky only lays between 90 to 120 eggs per year. They make excellent brood hens but in general, the Silkie is a chicken that is enjoyed more for their beauty and personality.

2. History of the Silkie

When we look at the history of the Silkie, we actually have to look back to Ancient China when the Silkie first appeared. One thing that should be mentioned is that the actual origin of the Silkie chicken is not known.

We do know that the Silkie chicken came from somewhere in Southeast Asia and that is may have come from India or Java. We also know that the first documentation of the Silkie chicken was when Marco Polo wrote about furry chickens in the 13 century. He came across the breed during his travels through Asia.

In addition, the breed was also described by Ulisse Aldorvandi, a naturalist at the University of Bologna when he published a treatise on chickens.

Despite having this knowledge on Silkies, how they made their way into Europe and North America is still uncertain. It is believed that the Silkie was imported to many countries through the Silk Route.

By 1984, the Silkie was officially recognized by North America and was accepted in the Standard of Perfection. The breed became very common in North America and Western Europe and became a popular breed as an ornamental fowl.

Today, the breed is still raised and celebrated as an ornamental breed, however, they are also commonly used as a brood hen to hatch out and raise anything from the young of other chickens to pheasants and even geese.

3. General Facts about the Silkie

Before we launch into the actual care of the Silkie, it is important to go over some of the general facts about the Silkie chicken. These questions will answer some of the more pressing questions about the breed and will help you in deciding if the Silky chicken is the right breed for you.

Do Silkies make good pets?

While the general answer is no, chickens in general are not pets in the traditional sense of the word, Silkies are a wonderful animal to have in your backyard.

They are usually very friendly and while they do not live inside, they will interact with people who visit their yard and coop on a daily basis. In addition, Silkies are usually very affectionate and enjoy being held and pet.

Are they a good pet for children to have?

Silkies tend to be very friendly to children; however, they are not an ideal pet for children. They can carry diseases that can pass to humans and they require special care that children cannot do.

That being said, backyard chickens, especially Silkies are wonderful to have around children. There have been cases of Silkies following children around like puppy dogs and they are docile, which makes them less scary to young children.

Why are they fluffy?

One of the most common questions that I am asked is why are Silkies fluffy. The main reason for this is due to the fact that the feather of the Silkie lacks barbicels. Barbicels are cartilage hooks that are on each hair of a feather. This leads to the feathers having a fur like appearance since the hairs fly free on the feather.

One thing that should be noted is that the Silkie feather is not a false feather or fur. It is actually a true feather and it functions in the same way that the feathers of other chicken breeds function.

Are they clean?

Silkie chickens are a livestock and with that comes some mess. They will peck at plants and other items around the yard and can be destructive if they are not properly cared for. In addition, they will shed feathers and you will need to clean up their coop and area on a regular basis to remove faeces.

Can they live in any enclosure?

No, Silkies need a coop to keep them warm and safe from predators. In addition, Silkies require a fenced yard or they will fall prey to predators such as raccoons and foxes.

Can Silkies live in any climates?

Yes, Silkies can live in a range of climates; however, they will need proper housing as well as heating when they live in colder climates.

It is important to note that Silkies do not have extra insulation due to their fur like feathers and will have the same protection from the cold as all other chickens.

Do you need special equipment for Silkie Chickens?

Yes, you will need some special equipment for your Silkie. This includes heating lamps, feeders and waterers and also a chicken coop. However, it is important to note that this is equipment that you would need for any type of chicken and the Silkie does not require any specialized equipment.

Are they good for someone new to chickens?

Due to their docile nature, Silkie chickens are an excellent chicken for those who are new to owning backyard chickens. They are usually easy to care for and since they do not wander or fly away, there isn't a lot of stress involved.

In addition, since they are amazing brood chickens, they are perfect for people who are just learning how to raise chickens from the egg since the Silkie will hatch and care for the chicks for you.

What is the lifespan of Silkie?

The actual lifespan of the Silkie will differ depending on the care that you give the bird. On average, Silkies live an average of 6 to 7 years. However, it is not unheard of for Silkies to live up to 13 years of age.

When you look at lifespan, we should also mention the laying lifespan on Silkies. On average, it is 2 to 3 years before you see a slow down to their egg laying, however, like lifespan, some Silkies will continue to lay eggs up until 5 years of age.

Are there different types of Silkie Chickens?

Yes, there are actually three different types of Silkies; however, the one type is not recognized in some countries. Specifically, type is identified by bearded and non bearded, which are two different Silkies. Bearded Silkies have a full face of feathers, while non-bearded do not.

The third type is the Bantam, which is ¼ to 1/5 the size of a standard sized Silkie. There are bearded and non bearded varieties of Bantam Silkies.

One thing that should be mentioned is that Silkies are also separated into colours, which I have gone over later on in this book.

How long do they take to mature?

Silkies are usually mature by about 6 months of age, which is the age when you start to see egg laying in hens and crowing behaviours in roosters.

Can Silkies be sexed at a young age?

Unfortunately, Silkies cannot be sexed at a young age. In fact, they are often not sexed until they are 6 months of age when you start to see laying behaviours in them. Some breeders can sex a Silkie earlier than 6 months; however, it is not 100% accurate.

Can you raise Silkies for meat and eggs?

Silkies are an ornamental breed, however, they can be used as meat and egg chickens. It is important to note that Silkies have black skin and bones, which makes them unappetizing to many, although they taste no different than other chicken breeds.

They are quite scrawny and do not have much body weight, making them less ideal for meat. In addition, they do not lay as frequently as other chicken breeds so they are not usually kept for laying. Finally, their eggs are usually smaller than an average egg.

Are Silkies good mothers?

If there is one question that gets a definitive yes, it is them being a good mother. Silkies are excellent brood chickens and they are often used to hatch and raise the young of other birds, including geese, other chickens and quail.

In addition, they work hard as mothers to young and are protective of their young. Silkies are so good as brood birds that even Silkie roosters will care for the young.

Can Silkies fly?

Since Silkies have a fluffy feather and one that is free of barbicels, they are not able to fly. They can jump but they are not strong jumpers.

Because of this, Silkies can do very well in yards that only have a 4 foot fence. However, they can be at risk to predators since they are so docile and are not able to jump away from the predator.

Do Silkies roost?

This differs depending on the individual Silkie. Some Silkies enjoy roosting; however, others do not enjoy it as much. When you create a roost, it is important to make the roost between 12 to 18 inches.

Do you need to groom your Silky?

If you are planning on raising Silkies for the chicken shows, then yes, you will need to do some special grooming for your chicken. I have gone over everything on the show Silkie later on in this book.

If you plan to simply enjoy the Silkie in your backyard, there isn't a lot of extra that needs to be done. You will need to do proper parasite control, but outside of that, the Silkie has a very easy to care for feather.

Do Silkies have 5 toes?

Yes, Silkies have 5 toes and this is known as polydactylism. The extra toe does not offer the Silkie any benefit but it is the breed standard.

Should you only have one rooster with the Silkie hens?

While it is common in many breeds to only have one rooster with their hens, Silkies are not one of those breeds. They are usually very docile and this makes them very gregarious to other males in the flock. It has been proven that Silkies can thrive in flocks with multiple males, although there is usually a more dominant male.

Are they noisy?

Silkies are no noisier than other chicken breeds; however, they can be noisy. Hens will cluck and make other noises through the day. In addition, Silkie roosters will crow and can be quite loud when they do.

Chapter 3. Anatomy of the Silkie

Before we get into the general care of your Silkie, it is important to understand the anatomy of a chicken in general and a Silkie specifically. The reason why this is important is because the more knowledge you have about your Silky, the better you are able to assess his or her health over the long run.

1. Silkie Anatomy

Although we can go into the anatomy of a chicken, which can be quite complex when you start to break it down, for this book, I want to just look at Silkie anatomy. What I mean by this is that I want to primarily look at what makes the Silkie so unique from other chicken breeds.

a) Feathers

Obviously, the first thing that we should talk about is the feathers of a Silkie. While other breeds have defined feathers, the Silkies feathers almost looks like the fur of a mammal and not an actual feather.

Before I go any further, I want to stress that Silkies have feathers that function in exactly the same way that other chicken feathers function. They do provide protection from the elements but they do not offer added protection. The only difference in function is that Silkies cannot fly at all, even short distances.

The other major difference with Silkie feathers is that the feather has a very silky texture to it, hence the name of the breed. This texture is due to the fact that the barbicels, which are small cartilage hooks on each hair of a feather, are not present in the Silkies feathers.

This means that the feathers do not sit straight and you lose the sleek look of the feathers because the hairs do not stick together.

With the feathers, a Silky should have feathers that grow on the legs and toes. In addition, the Silky should have a crest of feathers, looking like a top knot, on the top of its head. This is seen in both hens and roosters.

b) Skin, Bones and Meat

One thing that is often surprising with the Silky is the colour of the skin, bones and meat. Believe it or not, Silkies have dark gray to black skin, bones and meat. At this point, there is no known reason for this and it is unique in the Silkie breed.

While it may not look appetizing, Silkie flesh can be eaten, although they are rather scrawny birds and don't have a lot of flesh on them.

In China, where the Silky was originally developed, the meat of the Silkie has medicinal properties and is believed to help menstrual cramps, alleviate postpartum disorders, protect against feebleness, decrease anaemia, increase immunity and work as a treatment for diabetes. It is important to note that no research has been done to suggest any validity in these findings.

c) Toes and Wings

Another unique feature of the Silky is the fact that it has five toes. If you are not aware of this, most chicken breeds have four toes. Again, there is no known function for the fifth toe or reason why the Silkie chicken has five toes.

The wings of the Silkie are medium sized in comparison to their body. They do not function for flight and they sit quite far back on the Silkie's back.

d) Face

The final thing I am going to look at is the face of the Silkie. They actually have a very interesting face and while you can't see if in bearded Silkies, in the non-bearded Silkie, you can really enjoy it.

The first thing that you will notice on a Silkies face is that it is very smooth. The second thing is that it has the same gray-black colouring as the rest of its skin and feet.

The eyes of the Silkie are usually dark brown to almost black in colouring. They are quite large for a chicken. One of the more interesting features of the Silkies face is the earlobes, which are turquoise blue. In bearded Silkie chickens, you cannot see these earlobes.

Finally, Silkies have a curved beak that is thick and short and the comb of the Silkie looks very similar to a walnut.

2. The Colouring

Silkies are beautiful chickens that have a lot of wonderful colours to them. In fact, there are several different colours that you can find and all of them are as breathtaking as the last. While Silky breeders and enthusiasts may differentiate Silkies according to their colour, there is no difference in the type due to colour.

In addition, it is possible to breed different colours to each other, however, it is not recommended as it can be difficult to recreate the colours of the parents in crossbreeding. For that reason, they are usually bred to members of the same colour, creating a type, to keep the uniformed colours associated with the colour.

a) Blue

Blue is a wonderful colour and one of my personal favourites. It is not a bright blue but more of a blue slate colour. The head of the blue Silkie chicken should be black and the feathers should be glossy.

The hackles of the Silkie should be a bluish-black slate. In addition, the legs, breast and neck will also have the same bluish slate colouring; however, there should be black lacing through the feathers. Finally, the tail, back and saddle should be a clear colour, again, the same bluish slate; however, there should be glossy black markings on them.

Although you may see colour differences in other colour types, the blue silky does not have gender specific colouring and markings. Both males and females look similar.

b) White

The white Silky chicken is striking in appearance with the completely white body. Everything on the chicken should be white including the shafts of the feathers, the web and the fluff.

There is no difference in colouration or patterning between males and females.

c) Buff

Buff Silkies are the same as pure white Silkies in that there is no other colour on the animal. The entire Silky should be buff in colouring, which is yellowish beige. Again, this includes the shafts of the feathers, web and fluff.

There is no difference in colouration or patterning between males and females.

d) Black

While the black Silky is called black, it is actually quite colourful. The under colour of the feathers is usually a dull black, although dark legged varieties of this colour will have an under colour that matches their feathers. The plumage itself is a greenish-black in colour and the feathers should look lustrous.

There is very little difference in markings between males and females with black Silkies.

e) Partridge

Partridge Silkie chickens are one of the few colours that have a noticeable difference between the males and the females. The females are usually more subdued in colour than the males and have a reddish-bay colour with black markings and black pencilling.

With males, the red is a rich colour and has a black marking on the front of the neck. The back of the Silky rooster is a brilliant green with green-black markings.

The wings are tipped in black with a reddish-bay colour and the fluff of the wing should be primarily black with a red tinge. The toes and legs of the partridge Silky rooster should be black while the hackle should be a green-black with lustrous feathers.

f) Gray

Finally, the gray Silkie chicken is as beautiful as the other colours and can be a wonderful addition to any flock. They are usually a chinchilla gray and the roosters and hens have slightly different colouring and markings.

The hens are usually an even chinchilla gray with slate gray feathers on the head and hackle.

Roosters are a darker gray with a dark gray head and a light gray hackle with darker gray streaks. The under colour of the male is a smoky gray while the tail, shoulders and back is a chinchilla gray. There saddle of the rooster should match the hackle and the toes and shanks should be slate-blue in colouration.

And those are the colours that you will see. It is important to note that every type of Silkie can have these colours and later in this chapter, I will go over the types.

3. Sexing your Silkie

When it comes to sexing Silkies, you should be prepared for a challenge since Silkies are considered to be one of the hardest breeds to sex. The reason for this is because male and female Silky chickens share many of the same characteristics and this makes determining gender quite difficult.

With Silky chickens, sexing usually doesn't occur until the chick is close to 2 or 3 months of age. The older the chick is, the easier it is to tell the sex. When you are sexing your Silkie, there are a number of traits that you should look for and I will go over those in this section.

One: Streamers

Streamers are feathers that come off of the crest on a Silkie. These are only seen in male Silkies since females have a rounded crest. The streamers can be seen in your Silkie roosters between the ages of 4 to 6 months.

Two: Combs

When you are looking at your Silky, you should pay special attention to the walnut comb on their heads. While males and females have a walnut comb, males have a larger, more noticeable comb.

Three: Posture

While this isn't always a fool proof trait to look for, the majority of Silky rooster will hold their body's more erect than Silky hens will.

Four: Standing Watch

At a young age, usually around 4 months of age, a male Silkie will begin standing watch over the flock. What this means is that the watch over the hens in the flock, although they will be social to other males.

In addition to watching over their flock, males will guard their hens from predators and other threats.

Five: Hackle Feathers

The hackle feathers of a rooster are often rougher in texture than those of a female.

Six: Crowing

Finally, one of the best ways to determine sex is by the natural trait of males to start crowing. Males often begin growing around 4 to 6 months of age.

It is not an exact science but usually, just watching your chickens can help you determine the sex. Once they start laying, then it will be abundantly clear which Silkies are hens and which are roosters.

4. Types of Silkies

Now that we have explored as much about Silky chicken anatomy as we can in this book, it is time to look at the different types of Silkies that you can buy.

Before we do, however, it is important to note that in many countries, Silkies are known as Bantam Silkies. While there is a bantam variety, it is important to know what your country classifies as a bantam; it could simply be a standard sized Silky that you are purchasing.

While Bantam Silkies have set weights for their standard, it is important to note that there is no weight difference between bearded and non bearded Silkies. All standard sized Silkies should weigh up to 1.8kg for a male and 1.36kg for a female. They are a smaller type of bird.

a) Bearded Silkies

Bearded Silkies are often the type of Silkie that most people think of when they think of the breed. They are very similar to the non-bearded; however, the bearded have more feathers on their face.

Like all Silkies, the bearded Silky has a soft, hair like feather that leaves the chicken looking silky. This is due to the fact that the bearded silky does not have any barbicels and instead, have only down on their bodies.

With the bearded Silky, you should see a Silkie with a full beard. What this means is that your Silky should have a muff of feathers that cover the earlobes of the chicken. These feathers should then slow around and down the beak before turning horizontal to create a collar. This gives the beard three oval parts on the collar. In addition to the beard, they should have a topknot of feathers on the top of their head.

With bearded Silkies, the beard is a characteristic trait that is seen in both males and females. Bearded Silkies can be any of the colours that have been listed in the colour types.

b) Non Bearded Silkies

Non bearded Silkies look exactly like bearded Silkies, except they are missing the beard. Like the bearded, the non bearded Silkie has a soft, hair like feather that leaves the chicken looking silky. This is due to the fact that the bearded silky does not have any barbicels and instead, have only down on their bodies.

However, unlike the bearded, non bearded Silkies have no beard on their face. Instead, the earlobes, which are turquoise, are visible. Also visible is the wattle and the face of the non bearded.

Like all other Silkies, the non bearded Silky can be found in a range of colours, however, the face has a black pigmentation to it and the earlobes should be turquoise.

c) Bantams

The final type of Silkie that we will be going over is the Bantam Silkie. One thing that should be noted is that in many countries, full sized Silkies are often called Bantam Silkies. However, in other countries, the Bantam Silky is a distinct breed that is differentiated from other Silkies.

The only real difference between a Bantam Silky and a Silky is that the Bantam Silkie should be the actual size of the chicken. In general, Bantam Silkies are usually one-fourth to one-fifth the weight of a Silkie.

According to the Bantam breed standard, Bantam Silkies, regardless of whether they are bearded or non bearded, varies depending on where you are. In the American Standard of Perfection, the Bantam Silkie should be about 1kg in weight for a male and 907 grams for a female.

The British standard for the Bantam Silky should be 600 grams for males and 500 grams for a female. Finally, the Australian Poultry Standard for Bantam Silkies places the males at 680 grams and the females at 570 grams. These are the maximum weights that they should be.

In all other ways, including structure, shape, plumage and colouring, the Bantam Silkie is exactly like the regular Silkie. In addition, you can have Bearded Bantam Silkies and Non-Bearded Bantam Silkies.

And that is all you need to know about the anatomy of the Silkie.

Chapter 4. The Silkie Personality

If you ask anyone who has ever owned a Silky chicken what the best quality of the chicken is, they will tell you that it is their personality. In fact, there personality is so wonderful that they are often referred to as family pets before they are referred to as a laying, backyard chicken.

Through the years, I have owned a wide variety of backyard chickens and while they can all be entertaining to watch, the Silkie is an exceptional chicken.

While they are not the best breed to purchase when it comes to laying, Silkie chickens are not the best choice. They are known for laying a lower amount of eggs than other breeds. However, if you are looking for a brood hen, one that will hatch chicks, you can't go wrong with a Silkie.

In fact, Silkies are so patient with brooding that you can place any type of egg in their next, even larger eggs that take longer to incubate, and the Silkie will diligently sit on the next until the chick hatches out.

In addition to having the patients to be a champion brooder, the Silkie is known for its gentle nature. This is a chicken that is happy to simply peck around your backyard and they will often interact with people in the garden. This makes them a perfect addition to small backyard flocks where you don't have a lot of space.

In addition, they don't startle easily and are not birds that will be flighty. What this means is that you can simply work in your yard without the risk of your Silkie fluttering around you. In addition, most Silkies have no desire to escape their yard and you can easily keep Silkie chickens in yards with only a 4 foot fence.

Another bonus to having Silkies in your garden is that they are very gentle to the plants in your garden. Many Silkie chicken owners know that the chickens will actively seek out snails and other pests in your garden and when they do, they rarely destroy or damage the plant they pick the snails from.

In general, Silkies are a fun chicken to have in your flock. They can be very friendly with everyone, including children. They are very nurturing mothers to chicks and will even mother chicks that aren't their own.

They can be quite funny and it is very easy to teach a Silkie to accept your touch. Many Silkies actually enjoy being stroked and touched and this is often due to the fact that they are handled so much as chicks. Petting a Silky can be quite enjoyable because of their plumage.

On the day to day, a flock with a Silky is enjoyable and there are rarely fights between Silkies. They do need a little extra care as they are not always that graceful and will often need to be picked up when they are put away in the coop for the night.

In addition, they don't seem to do well with protecting themselves from predators or other chickens. Often, they become easy prey for predators due to their docile nature. In addition, if there are other breeds of chickens in the flock, Silkies are often bullied by the other chickens. For that reason, it is important to keep your Silkies separated as much as possible.

With free roaming, the Silkie is an amazing breed. They are happy to stay in a small garden or yard and won't try to escape if there is a small fence. In addition, they are not overly aggressive and roosters and hens will mix in the flock easily without too many problems.

Chapter 5. Preparing for your Silkie

So it is an exciting time for you. By now, you have probably decided on bringing home your very own Silkie and this can be quite exciting. However, before you bring home your Silky, it is important to create a safe place for your chicken.

In this chapter, I will go over everything you need to know before you bring your Silkie home.

1. Purchasing your Silkie

Purchasing a Silkie can actually be a very trying task when you are first getting into the breed. One of the main reasons for this is that people aren't sure where to go. Often, local breeders only focus on meat or egg laying chickens. They do not have the ornamental breeds.

That being said, you can still find many sources on line and even eBay has Silkies that you can purchase. One of the first things I will recommend to anyone is to contact their local Silkie club to find out where they can find a Silkie on its own.

With Silkies, it is important to note that you should consider whether you want to purchase young adults or if you want to bring home eggs and raise the chicks. You can do both but I recommend that you read the chapter on breeding chickens, specifically the sections on eggs and hatchlings.

When you purchase a Silkie, make sure that you are purchasing from a breeder of purebred Silkies. There are Silkie breeders out there that are crossing Silkies with other breeds and this can affect the feather type that you get.

In addition, the general rule of thumb is that you should always purchase at least 3 Silkies since this is a sociable chicken that enjoys being in a flock. A single Silkie will become lonely and it will affect her health.

When you have found a Silkie breeder, take the time to find out about the laws in your area. Are you allowed to have chickens? Do you need a permit? Some areas require special permits for keeping backyard chickens of any type and some areas have full bans on backyard chickens.

In addition to local laws, make sure that you check with your neighbours before you purchase any type of backyard fowl. While it may be a delight for you, chickens can be quite loud, especially if you have a rooster.

Offer your neighbours fresh eggs and you will be sure to win them over quickly and easily.

Once you have done all of those things, you can simply bring your Silkies home and begin enjoying them on a daily basis.

2. Setting up a Coop and Run for your Silkie

In general, the Silkie is not a very demanding poultry. They are very happy in a small coop and run and only require about 2 square feet of space per chicken. I would recommend giving them more room that that and if you have the proper yard and garden, let them free range in your yard instead of just in the run.

One thing that should be mentioned is that if you are raising a show Silkie, you will need to have more room for them to prevent damage to the feathers.

With coop selection, you should look for a coop and run that is connected. There are many on the market that can be perfect for a Silkie, especially if you are only keeping a small coop.

In general, there really is no difference in the type of coop that you can purchase. Silkies are low maintenance chickens and they don't require a lot of extras in the coop. With any breed of chicken, your coop should have the following traits:

Protection:

A coop should offer protection from both the weather and predators. It should be kept behind a fenced area that predators cannot get into.

In addition, it should block out winds and should be resistant to rain and snow. One thing that should be pointed out is that coops do not have to be insulated even in northern climates. However, if you have insulation in your coop, make sure that it is sealed in the walls. Silkies will peck insulation and it can make them very sick.

Fencing:

This ties hand in hand with protection but make sure that you have a fence around the run. This fence should be high enough so the chickens cannot jump out.

Silkies are not big jumpers but they can jump about 3 to 4 feet, however, there are predators that a 4 foot fence won't keep them

out so it is better to have a higher fence around your run. If you are not sure what a run is, it is the outside yard where the chickens can scratch and be outside.

In addition to the fencing, it is important to place a hardware cloth in the ground. This should attach to the bottom of the fence and go into the ground 12 inches. By doing this, you can prevent the predators from going under the fence and attacking your Silkies.

With fencing, make sure that it is the proper size for the age of your chickens. Chicks require chick fencing so they can't slip through the fence. Chickens can use any type of fencing.

Ventilation:

It is very important that your coop has good ventilation. The main reason for this is that chicken droppings do have a lot of ammonia in them. This ammonia, if it builds in the chicken coop, can cause respiratory problems in your Silkies.

Lighting:

Lighting is another important item that you should have in your coop. Chickens that don't have proper lighting will stop laying or slow down laying in the winter months.

In addition, in colder locations, you can add a heat lamp to a chicken coop to provide enough warmth during the winter. Make sure all heat lights are kept to the side so that the chickens can move away from the heat.

Nesting Boxes:

Since you want your Silkies to lay eggs and to nest, it is important to have nesting boxes in your coop. Many commercially built coops have nesting boxes, however, if you are building your own, you can use cola crates. You can also purchase nesting boxes for your coop.

Roost Poles:

Roost poles are not always necessary for Silkies since they do not roost frequently. If you want to have roosts, they should only be 12 inches up as Silkies are not jumpers. It is better to have roost poles that are about 1 foot apart and to give each bird about 1 foot to roost on.

For warmth, arrange the poles in a flat line, like a bed, since this will offer more warmth to the Silkies when they are roosting.

And that is all you need to know about your housing. There really is no right or wrong way to place your coop so simply find a place in your yard where you would like it and set it up.

3. Supplies for your Silkie

The final thing that I want to talk about regarding getting ready for your Silkie is your actual equipment that you will need. While it may seem like you will need a lot, if you are simply raising chickens and not breeding, you don't actually need much. If you are breeding, you will need the equipment and supplies I have gone over in the chapter on breeding.

That being said, you will still need a few supplies and these are:

Feed:

It is important to provide your Silkies with a good quality commercial feed. Some breeders will make their own feed; however, nutrition is very important for your Silkies so I recommend a commercially formulated feed.

Bedding:

Every nest box should have bedding and you can use a range of them. I recommend pine shavings since they don't encourage pest infestations as much as other bedding; however, you can use stray and hay for bedding for your Silkies.

Waterer:

Although you can purchase waterers that rest on the floor, I recommend ones that hang so you don't have as much dirt, shavings and faeces in the waterer.

The general rule with waterers is to have 96 inches of trough space for 100 birds. Obviously, if you have only 2 or 3 Silkies, one waterer is enough to keep your Silkies well hydrated.

Sand:

You can place the sand in a dry spot in your run or you can put it into a bucket that the Silky can get into. The sand is used as a dust bath and should be out for the Silkies to use on a daily basis.

Feeder:

As with the waterer, you want a feeder, which is a specially designed feeding dish for chickens, that hangs and is up off of the ground.

Generally, you want 300 inches of trough space for every 100 birds and again, one feeder is enough for 2 or 3 birds.

Grit:

Grit is small stones, shells and gravel that chickens swallow to properly grind up the food that they are given. If they free range, you don't need to provide as much grit as they will pick up stones on their own, however, if they don't, this is a must have supply for your Silkies.

And that is all the supplies that you really need for your Silkies.

Chapter 6. The Show Chicken World

One of the main reasons that people purchase Silkies is to take them into the world of show competitions and it is actually a very interesting and popular thing to do.

For those that are not aware of what shows for chickens are, it is actually an exhibition where pure breed chickens are judged according to a standard set up for that bird.

With exhibiting, you can earn points to produce a champion bird. If you are a breeder of show poultry, this helps your program; however, there is a unique pride to owning your very own champion.

While it may seem like a difficult endeavour, starting out in the show chicken world is actually quite easy and anyone who has a purebred chicken can enter.

1. Preparing to Show

One of the most important things that you can do for a show chicken is to prepare it for a show. While this means that you will need to get it used to grooming, I will go over that later in this chapter.

Instead, when I mention preparing to show, it is important to take the time to familiarize yourself with the Silky breed standard and the ins and outs of showing.

Generally, a show for chickens requires you to register prior to the actual event. Once you have registered, you will receive a show schedule that will give you all the important information about the show.

On the day of the show, you simply transport your Silkie, tidy him or her up and pen him. Then you let the judges do their thing and judge the chicken.

Unlike other shows, such as shows for dogs, you do not have to walk the chicken around a ring or anything. The judges will make their own choices while you enjoy the sights and sounds of the show.

One thing that is very important to mention is that you should condition your Silkie to being penned. If a Silkie is going to be shown, he will need to be in the pen. All that needs to go into pen training is simply placing them into a pen every day to help condition them to it.

Also make sure that you gradually increase the noise of the area the penning occurs in. This will help keep your Silkie from tightening up and not allowing you to really show him off in the best popular way.

The next thing you should do is start getting the Silkie used to being handled. Hopefully, if you have had him or her since the Silkie was a chick, handling is not an issue. The reason why you want the chicken to become used to being handled is that judges will pull the bird from the pen to get a good look at the chicken and judge it fairly.

If the Silkie is agitated with being handled, it will not show well and the stress will actually cause it to tighten its feathers and not appear as fluffy as it should.

Finally, another trick that is important for preparing for shows is to train your Silkie to follow a stick. You can do this by placing tempting treats on the end of the stick and then having the Silkie follow it.

While it may seem like a strange trick, judges will use sticks to move the chickens around to see them display. By training the Silkie to display, you will have a better chance of owning a champion bird.

2. Grooming Your Silkie

Although grooming can be general care of a Silkie, often, chicken owners do not groom their Silkie unless they are attending a show. For that reason, I have included it in this chapter.

In general, grooming is very easy for a Silkie and there are only a few things that you will need to do, which I will go through in this section.

a) Bathing your Silkie

Bathing a Silkie is not necessary for day to day care since Silky chickens will use dust baths to keep their feathers clean and free of pests. However, if you are planning on attending a show, you will need to groom your silky for it.

With bathing, you can use a mild baby shampoo for the feathers. This will keep the feathers looking good without drying out the skin of the chicken. In addition to the baby shampoo, you should use a dog shampoo that is specific to your Silkie's colour. For instance, if you have a black Silkie, choose a shampoo for black dogs.

Finally, you will need vinegar for bathing your Silky.

Once you have all the supplies, follow these steps:

Step One: Wet the Silky Down

Place the Silkie in a sink and with warm water, carefully wet her down. Be sure to get the entire bird and not just her back.

Step Two: Shampoo with Baby Shampoo

Once she is wet, pour baby shampoo onto the Silkie. Work the shampoo into the feathers and be sure to do the head, and beard if it is a bearded Silky.

In addition, scrub the toes, feet and make sure that you pay extra attention to the vent area where there can be some faeces stuck to the feathers.

Step Three: Rinse

Once you have scrubbed your Silkie completely, rinse out the baby shampoo. Make sure that you get all of the shampoo out as you don't want to have any irritants in the feathers and on the skin.

Step Four: Apply Second Shampoo

Apply the dog shampoo that has been developed for colour to your Silkie. Rub the shampoo in and make sure that it is worked into the entire chicken.

Once it is worked in, leave it in for 3 to 5 minutes. You can use dog shampoo for white dogs on all of the colours, however, if you do, use the shorter time limit or you will wash out the colour of your Silky and make the colour look dull.

Step Five: Rinse

After the allotted time, rinse the Silkie out completely with warm water.

Step Six: Apply Vinegar

After the shampoo is rinsed out, mix 2 cups of water with 2 tablespoons of vinegar and stir until it is well blended.

Pour the vinegar solution over the Silkie and scrub the bird as you are pouring. You will actually find that there is still shampoo in the feathers. The vinegar will remove the last of it.

Step Seven: Final Rinse

After you have rinsed out the Silkie with the vinegar, rinse the Silkie one last time with water until the vinegar has been rinsed out.

Step Eight: Dry your Silkie

After the bath, make sure that you dry your Silkie. Wring out the feathers as best you can. After that, wrap the Silkie into a towel tightly.

While they are wrapped in the towel, you can do the other grooming of your Silkie. When it is ready to be dried, use a low powered grooming dryer to dry the Silkie completely. An added bonus is the dryer will fluff out your Silkies feathers.

b) Nail Trimming

As I mentioned in the section on bathing, it is better for both you and your bird to have them wrapped in a towel when you do the nail trimming. This will keep them secure and will also minimize the stress of a nail trim.

Supplies that you will need for trimming the nails of your Silkie are:

- Cornstarch or Styptic Powder
- Nail Clippers
- Nail File

To trim your Silkies nails, follow these steps:

Step One: Inspect the Foot

Nail trimming is a perfect opportunity to look at your Silkies feet. Look for any damage on the foot that may require medical attention.

When you are inspecting the foot, check where the quick, which is the vein in the nail, is.

Step Two: Support the Foot

After you have inspected the foot, grasp it in your hand and support the entire foot. Do not hold the toe that you are planning on trimming as this will cause stress and/or pain to your Silkie.

Step Three: Clip the Nail

Select a nail to trim and cut the nail across the nail. To avoid cutting the quick, you can make short cuts and slowly move up the nail.

If you accidentally cut the quick, you will see blood on the end of the nail. Dip the nail into styptic powder or cornstarch, this will stop the bleeding.

Step Four: File the Rough Edges

Before you move onto the next nail, check for any rough edges on the nail. If there is a rough edge, file it with a nail file or emery board until it is smooth.

Step Five: Repeat

Repeat steps three and four on all of the other toes on that foot. Grasp the other foot securely and repeat steps three and four on the second foot.

c) Filing the Beak

Like I mentioned with nail trimming, you will want to have your Silkie secured in a towel with this. Beak trimming can be done with showing; however, it is also good to do with chickens in your flock to prevent pecking.

With trimming, you will need the following supplies:

- Dog Nail Clippers
- Cornstarch or Styptic Powder
- Nail File

To trim your Silkies beak, follow these steps:

Step One: Inspect your Chicken's Face

Before you do any trimming, you want to take the time to look at the actual face and beak of your Silkie. Look for any signs of disease or injury that may need medical treatment.

Once you have done that, try to see the quick. Like the nail, chicken beaks have a quick that is a vein in the beak. If it is clipped it will bleed.

Step Two: Clip the Upper Beak

After you have inspected the face and beak, start clipping the beak. It is better is you start with small clippings since you don't want to cut into the quick.

You want to clip just the top half of the beak, or the upper beak, and usually, you are working on only the white part of the beak.

Clip the beak with a square cut. Trim the beak back until it is slightly longer than the bottom beak, or lower half of the beak.

If you hit the quick, dip it in cornstarch or styptic powder to stop the bleeding.

Step Three: File the Beak

Once it is trimmed down, take your nail file and round out the edges to shape the beak back to its natural shape.

Step Four: Apply Baby Oil

After the beak has been trimmed and filed, you can add baby oil to the beak to make it look shiny.

And that is really all you need to do with your Silkie to get it ready for show or to groom it on a regular basis.

Chapter 7. Caring for your Silkie

Once you have your Silkie chicken at home, there isn't a lot that you need to do except enjoy the chickens as they go about their day.

Silkies are a very social animal and it can be enjoyable to watch them as they bob and weave through your garden. They do have their own personalities and often, Silkies endear themselves to their owner's hearts.

One thing that should be emphasized is that you should not over crowd your chickens. A small hen house should house only two or three chickens and generally, you want to make sure that they have two square feet of space per every Silky that you have in your coop.

During the first few days that you have your Silkies at home, you will find that they Silkies will establish the pecking order of the flock. This is actually very common and not something to be alarmed about. The only thing that you should be worried about is if one or two Silkies are being bullied for several days with no signs of it getting better.

In general, however, Silkies usually get along well with each other and are not prone to fighting. They are usually quite docile and this often makes them easy to bully by other chickens, which is why they should not be kept in a mixed flock.

On the day to day, there really isn't a lot that needs to go into the care of your Silkies, except it is important to do the following for daily care:

1. Wash out the water dishes.
2. Fill them with fresh water and add half a cup of Apple Cider Vinegar.

3. Place out the fresh water for the chickens and check it several times per day.
4. Replace the dust bath if necessary.
5. Add grit to the grit feeder.
6. Fill the feeders with the feed for the day. See the chapter on feeding to determine the best way to feed.
7. Remove any dirty straw from the coop.
8. Turn the chickens out into their run or into the yard.
9. Pick up the feeders at night.
10. Wash out the feed containers and dry completely.
11. Put the Silkies back into the coop for the night.

And that is pretty much all you need to do on a daily basis. Most of the care is simply keeping them fed and watered through the day.

The only other thing that you will need to do is sweep up feathers and dirt and wash off any feces in the nesting areas. In addition, collect the eggs. The collecting of eggs differs depending on the individual. Some people prefer to collect the eggs once a day, others several times a day.

Before we close this chapter, however, I want to leave you with a few tips for caring for your Silkie throughout its life.

Tip Number One: Handle your Silkie often

This should start when your Silky is young since the more you handle it, the tamer it will be. Silkies are very easy to tame and they enjoy being handled so start the process as soon as your Silkies come home.

While this may not seem like a big tip, it is one that can save you a lot of problems. Silkies that enjoy being held can be checked easily for illnesses, groomed for shows and administering treatments as needed.

Tip Number Two: Check your Security

On a daily basis, I recommend doing a visual sweep of your fence to make sure that there are no signs of wear and tear. Silkies, while not prone to wandering, can escape if there is a hole in the

fence. In addition, predators will quickly take advantage of weaknesses in your fencing.

Another thing that you should check weekly is the hardware cloth. If you haven't placed this around your fence, bury half inch hardware cloth for about 12 inches below the chicken run or fence. This will help prevent predators from digging under the fence. Even if you have it, always check the cloth to make sure no digging has been done. A persistent predator will dig down and pry up that cloth.

Tip Number Three: Give treats to your Silkie

Another tip is to give your Silkie some treats. This will offer them some extra nutrition and is a great way to spoil your Silky – just be sure that you don't spoil them too much. In the chapter on feeding.

Tip Number Four: Keep your Flock the Same Age

Another tip that will help alleviate your care is to keep the age of your flock similar. This will help alleviate feeding complications and will also curb bullying of other chickens. Actually, one of the main reasons for bullying behaviours in Silkies and chickens is when there are smaller, weaker members in the flock.

Having birds that are all close to the same age and size will help reduce a lot of stress for your birds and will result in you having less care to deal with in regards to injuries and feeding.

Tip Number Five: Enjoy your Silkies

One thing that can often be forgotten on the day to day is that owning chickens, especially Silkies, can be an enjoyable thing. Silkies are personable, affectionate and funny and you can spend hours sitting on the deck watching your Silkie go about his or her business.

As I mentioned, caring for a Silkie is very easy and you don't have to do a lot of extra.

Chapter 8. Feeding your Silkie

When it comes to feeding your Silkie, there really isn't a lot that you need to know. Silkie chickens will eat the same way that other breeds of chickens will eat and if they are free ranging, many of their needs, such as pebbles and plants, will be taken care of when they are ranging.

In this chapter, I will go over everything you need to know about feeding your Silky so you can ensure that she stays healthy.

1. Tips for Feeding

The very first thing that every chicken owner should learn is the tips for properly feeding your chickens. These are important as they will help you establish good habits that will ensure the lifelong health of your Silkie.

It is important to mention, before we get into the tips, that feeding Silkies is not exact. Some chickens will need to be fed different amounts of feed due to the age and whether they are laying or not.

In general, if you are looking at laying hens, you will want to feed your Silkie hen about 4 pounds of feed for every dozen eggs that the hen produces. In addition, you usually feed 2 pounds of feed for every pound of weight that you want your Silkie to gain.

While we are looking at large numbers, you do not actually feed each hen 4 pounds at every feeding. This will only lead to much of the food being wasted.

Instead, you should feed a laying Silkie hen about ¼ pound of feed every day to make sure that they are getting enough. A male can be fed the same amount. Remember to watch your Silkie chickens to make sure that they maintain a good body weight and to ensure that they stay healthy. If you suspect that you are not feeding your Silkies enough, adjust the amount of feed you give your chickens.

Now that you understand the amount, let's look at the tips for feeding your Silky chickens.

Tip Number One: Adjust Food According to Weather

Believe it or not, chickens need their food levels adjusted depending on the time of year and the weather outside. In general, Silkies will eat more food when it is cold outside and less food when it is hot. For that reason, make sure you adjust the amount of food that you are giving your Silkies according to the temperature. It may only be a slight shift but it will make the difference, especially in colder months.

Tip Number Two: Always Have Access to Water

Clean drinking water is important for Silkies and you should offer them fresh, clean water every day. Make sure you place it in a chicken friendly waterer and refill it several times per day as needed.

Tip Number Three: Allow the Chickens to Feed Themselves

While you can feed your chickens twice a day, I find that it is better to use a dish or a feeder to feed the chickens throughout the day. Generally, Silkies like to eat small amounts of food throughout the day so it is better to allow them to choose when to eat.

That being said, it is important to pick up any feed at the end of the day that wasn't eaten. Empty out the feeders and place them in a pest safe place for the night. Leaving it out can lead to pests or mold in your feed, which can cause health problems for your Silkie.

Tip Number Four: Offer them a Variety

While you will need to stick with a nutritional blend of feed, it is important to offer them some variety through plants and other treats. Later in this chapter, I will go over a range of different treats that you can give your Silkies to ensure that they get a well rounded diet.

Tip Number Five: Offer Grit to your Silkies

Finally, be sure to offer grit, which is a mixture of limestone and granite, to your Silkies on a regular basis. If they are free ranging, you won't have to offer it as much as Silkies will pick up small pebbles, shells, bone, etc. as they scratch around.

The reason for grit is so the chicken has the ability to digest its food. Without grit, the food remains undigested and can lead to many problems.

When you do feed grit, make sure that you offer it after the chickens have eaten. Young chickens and chicks will eat a large quantity of grit and actually fill up on grit instead of feed.

In addition to feeding it after they have eaten, make sure that you offer it in a small, narrow feeder. Chickens will have dust baths in grit and this can promote the spread of disease and illness if the Silkie defecates in the grit.

And those are all the tips that you need to know about feeding. Now it is time to move on to the types of feed you can offer your Silkies.

2. Types of Food

With feeding, the type of food that you offer your Silkie is no different than the type of food that you offer any chicken. Silkies do not need any special nutrition so don't worry about feeding all the chickens in your flock, regardless of breed, the same feed.

When you look at a feed, you want to find a high quality feed. While many breeders and chicken farmers will make their own feed, it is important to avoid this if you are new to chickens. Chickens require set nutritional levels and when you make your own feed, it is very easy to miss those levels.

Although many people don't pay much attention to the form that the feed comes in, it is important for the health of your Silkie that you do. With feed, you can purchase it in three forms and those are:

- *Crumbles:*
Crumbles are a feed
where you have a
range of different
sized grains
together. They are
actually one of the
best foods that you
can feed to your
Silkies and research
has proven that you
see better growth
and laying when a
Silkie is on
crumbles.

- *Pellet:* Pellets are very similar to pellets you would purchase for a rabbit and many chicken farmers use them. If you cannot find a crumble in your area, then I would recommend a pellet. However, you should limit your pellet use to only adult Silkies.

- *Mash:* Mash is a feed that has an oatmeal like texture to it and you will need to add water to the mash. It is excellent as a starter food; however, it is not one that I recommend for adult Silkies. For one, you cannot leave it for too long or it will begin to spoil. From my experience, Silkies love mash and will eat it quickly; however, it is not as high quality as a crumble or pellet.

Now that you know the forms the feed can come in, let's look at the different types of feed that you can purchase.

Starter Rations:

Starter rations are an excellent food that is commonly used for

chicks from the time they are born until they are 6 weeks of age. There are actually several different types of starter rations with higher and lower levels of protein. With Silkies, you want to choose a protein ratio of about 20% since they are not meat chickens.

Another option with starter rations is to choose one that has medication in it. This will help protect your chicks from a range of illnesses and diseases that can affect them.

Grower Rations:

The next type of feed that you can purchase for your Silkies is grower's rations. Again, these should be purchased in a lower protein level since Silkies are not raised for meat. Instead, choose a grower ration that is about 18% protein.

The grower ration is necessary for chicks and young chickens that are 6 to 14 weeks of age. This will help get them into peak condition for laying.

Finishing Rations:

Also known as developer rations, finishing rations is a feed that has a good level of vitamins and minerals, specifically calcium, that will help initiate laying in your chickens.

It should be fed to chickens from 15 week until they are 22 weeks old. In addition, you should make sure that it only has a 16%

protein ratio as you want your Silkies to gain a good weight but not too much fat.

Adult Rations:

By the time your Silkies have reached 22 weeks of age, they are ready to be placed on adult rations. These are rations that you will feed throughout their life.

Adult rations are usually 16 to 18% protein and it is important to only choose foods with this protein ratio. Too much protein is not good for laying birds; however, meat birds will need a 20% protein ratio.

Choose a commercial feed that has several different grains to make sure that it has the best nutrients for your Silkies.

Sweet Feed:

Sweet feed, or all stock as it is commonly known as, is a feed that is more of a treat and should not be given to the Silkies as a staple food. It is a mixture of whole grains, or a pellet, that is covered with a sweetener such as molasses. It is something that farm animals enjoy, however it offers no real nutrients.

And those are the feeds that you should be looking at. Remember to match the feed to the age of your Silkie to ensure that it receives the perfect nutrition.

3. Treats for your Silkie

As I mentioned in the last section, Silkies love to have treats and you should work treats into the everyday enjoyment of your chickens.

With treats, it is important to offer them in moderation and to not make the treat the staple of your Silkie's diet. In addition, watch your chickens. If you find the Silkies have any signs of digestion problems such as constipation or diarrheal, then stop giving your Silkie that treat.

Another thing to remember is that Silkies can be picky birds when they want to be and you will need to figure out what your Silkie chicken likes to eat through trial and error. Below is a list of treats that you can offer your Silkie.

Treat	Comments
Apple	Feed apples raw or as an applesauce. I recommend that you remove the core since apple seeds do contain cyanide.
Asparagus	Asparagus can be fed either raw or cooked; however, raw is a little easier for the chicken to peck apart.
Bananas	These are an excellent treat and they are a good source of potassium for your Silkies.
Beets	Feed your Silkies both the greens and the root.
Berries	Again, you can feed the fruit and the greens from berries. Silkies enjoy a wide range of berries and there are often no side effects to them.
Breads	Any type of bread can be fed to chickens, however, they are a starchy food and you want to minimize the amount of starch you feed your Silkies. Only give this treat occasionally.
Broccoli	This treat is also very good for Silkies and can be fed on a regular basis.
Cabbage	Any type of cabbage or vegetable belonging to the cabbage family, such as Brussels sprouts, is a good food for Silkies. You can hang it up where the Silkies can play with it as they peck it to alleviate any boredom the bird has.
Carrots	Give your Silkies both the actual carrot and the carrot greens. You can also give them cooked carrots if you prefer.
Cauliflower	See broccoli
Cereal	Since cereals are grains, you can use them as a treat for your Silkies; however, I don't recommend them

	as many cereals contain high levels of sugar, which is not recommended for Silkies.
Cheese	This includes cream cheese, cottage cheese and any other type of cheese you can buy. I am not a big fan of cheese as it can be quite fatty and it can cause stomach upset. However, other Silkie breeders have seen no problems with it. If you feed cheese, do so in moderation.
Cherries	Cherries are like berries and can make an excellent treat for your Silkies.
Corn	Corn is an excellent treat and you can give it to them on or off the cob. You can also feed it to them raw or cooked.
Crickets	If your Silkies are free range, then you will probably allow them to hunt for their own bugs, however, purchasing live crickets from a pet store can give them an opportunity for crickets on a more regular basis. Crickets are an excellent source of protein and do provide your Silkies, and you, with some entertainment.
Cucumbers	While you can feed your Silky cucumbers, it is better to choose overripe cucumbers so the Silky has access to seeds.
Eggplant	Another excellent treat, I recommend using overripe eggplant for softer flesh.
Flowers	Free ranging Silkies will often find flowers to eat and they can be quite the pest to your flower garden. They can eat a range of flowers, however, make sure that they are not poisonous and that they are free of pesticides before you feed them to your Silkie.
Grains	Like cereal, you can choose from a wide range of grains to feed your Silkie and they will eat just about any type of grain. Some excellent choices are flax, wheat berries and oats.
Grapes	Only feed seedless grapes to your Silkies and cut them up to prevent choking.
Lettuce	Lettuce is an excellent treat that you can give Silkies on a regular basis. It includes any type of lettuce from Iceberg to Kale.
Mealworms	Like crickets, mealworms have a good level of

	protein and are a treat that many Silkies love. You can purchase them at pet stores very easily.
Melon	This also includes watermelon, cantaloupe and honey dew, melon can be cut and given to your Silkies. They can enjoy the seeds and the flesh of the melon.
Peaches	Peaches are a soft fruit that is an excellent treat. It does have a lot of sugar so don't feed it too frequently.
Pears	Like apples, pears are an excellent treat for your Silkie. Again, cut them up and remove the seeds.
Peas	Any type of pea is an excellent treat and you can give it to them in the pod. In addition, Silkies love the tendrils and flowers of peas.
Peppers	Only offer your Silkie bell peppers that are sweet. Never given your Silkies hot peppers.
Pomegranates	Pomegranates make an excellent treat for your Silky and all you need to do is crack it open for them to get at the seeds.
Popcorn	When you give popcorn, make sure that you only give air popped. Make sure there are no oils, butters or salts on it.
Potatoes	These can make an okay treat, however, you should only give cooked and cut out the green parts of the potato as that can be poisonous. I do not recommend potatoes as a frequent treat since they have high levels of starch.
Raisins	Raisins do contain a high level of sugar so they should only be offered in moderation.
Rice	Never feed your Silkie raw rice. Instead, offer it to your chickens cooked or not at all. Even cooked, it should only be offered in moderation.
Scratch	You will hear the term scratch often in the chicken world. It is actually a treat with multiple grains; however, it is not a feed as it doesn't have everything you need for your Silkie's nutrition. It is better for colder months.
Squash	Squash as well as pumpkin, is a popular treat with Silkies and they can eat both the flesh and seeds of the vegetable.

Sunflower Seeds	Sunflower seeds are an excellent treat for Silkies, especially egg laying hens as it encourages laying. In addition, it helps with the development of healthy feathers.
Tomatoes	Silkies love tomatoes and they will often go after tomato plants when they are looking for treat.
Table scraps	Yes, Silkies will eat table scraps and while it can be tempting to feed your Silky a table scrap, don't. Table scraps contain high levels of salt and other ingredients that can be harmful to your Silkie.
Yogurt	You can use both plain and flavoured yogurt with Silkies. Yogurt is actually very good for Silkies and helps with digestive health.

Now that you know the feed and the treats you can give your Silkies, there isn't much else that you need to remember. For many birds that are free range, treats aren't as important as they will find their own; however, I still recommend them so you can monitor their nutritional intake.

Chapter 9. Illnesses and Health

In this chapter, I will go over everything you need to know to keep your Silkie happy and healthy. Although it isn't always that difficult, Silkies and all other breeds of chickens are susceptible to a wide range of health problems and risk.

For that reason, it is important to study this chapter, where I have gone over the various conditions your Silkies can acquire and to pay close attention to your chickens. Catching an illness quickly can make the difference between recovery and death.

1. Keeping Your Silkie Healthy

Before we get into all the different diseases that your Silkie can have, it is important to look at some ways to keep your Silkie healthy. This often comes down to some important tips that you should follow.

Tip Number One: Disinfect the Coop

The very first thing that I recommend is that you keep your chicken coop clean and disinfect it on a weekly basis. If you are keeping up with cleaning, it shouldn't take too long to clean it.

When you disinfect your coop, you want to start by washing all the surfaces of the coop with soap and water. Allow it to dry before you wash the area with a disinfectant.

It is better to use a warm disinfectant since they are more effective then disinfectants that are cold. In addition, you should always let the disinfectant to sit on the surface for at least 30 minutes before you wash it off. This will ensure that any disease or bacteria is killed.

Tip Number Two: Always Provide Water

Make sure that your Silkies have constant access to fresh, clean water. Every night, wash out the water dishes to make sure that there is no bacteria or dirt in the water dishes. Place them back out for your chickens after they are cleaned.

Another great tip with water is to add a small amount of Apple Cider Vinegar to the water; this will help keep the chicken's pH levels at a healthy level.

Tip Number Three: Keep your Flock Closed

I have mentioned this before but it is important to keep your flock closed to prevent the spread of disease and to keep your Silkies healthy.

What keeping your flock closed means is that you do not bring in new stock without quarantining them first. In addition, you try to prevent contact between your flock and other wild birds. By doing this, you can reduce the risk of diseases coming into your flock.

Tip Number Four: Do a Daily Health Check

With your Silkies, it is very important to catch diseases quickly before they have a chance to spread to other chickens in your flock. Generally, look for signs of stress on your Silkies. Check for fatigue, diarrheal and also for difficulty moving. In addition, make sure eyes are bright, the nose and vent are clear of any debris and check the health of the feathers.

If there are no outward signs of disease, then you can let the Silkies enjoy the day. However, if you notice any signs of illness, make sure you quarantine that chicken to make sure that nothing is wrong with them.

Tip Number Five: Provide Dust Baths

Dust baths are shallow spots of sand or dirt where the Silkies can dig in and shake dust onto their skin and feathers. It is the equivalent of a shower and it will help remove a lot of parasites that may be trying to take hold in their feathers.

In addition to these tips, make sure that you feed them a high quality feed and to minimize treats. While treats can be healthy, you don't want to give them a treat daily as it can lead to stomach upset and poor nutrition.

2. Common Diseases

Despite giving your Silkies the very best care, there is still a risk of your chicken becoming infected with a number of diseases. One thing that is important to note is that many chicken diseases can be zoonotic. What this means is that the disease can be transmitted from the animal to the person or vice versa.

For that reason, it is imperative that you stay on top of the health of your Silkie. If you suspect an illness or see signs of disease, administer treatment or seek veterinarian care for your Silkie as soon as possible.

There are many diseases that your Silky chicken can be susceptible to and I will go over the most common diseases that you can see.

a) Infectious Bronchitis

Infectious bronchitis is a respiratory disease that is quite common in backyard flocks. It is also known as a cold and can be mild to severe depending on the natural immunity of the flock and the conditions in which they live.

Symptoms:

Like many respiratory illnesses, symptoms can often be confused with other conditions. Symptoms of infectious bronchitis include:

- Coughing
- Decrease or Cessation of Laying
- Discharge from Nose
- Discharge from Eyes
- Sneezing

Cause:

Infectious bronchitis is a viral disease that can affect chickens of any age. It is spread through contact with infected chickens. In addition, it can be spread through contact with contaminated surfaces. It is important to note that it is highly contagious and is also an airborne illness.

Treatment:

There is no treatment for infectious bronchitis outside of ensuring the chickens are comfortable. Keeping them in warm, dry areas and providing them with food and water will help them overcome the condition. It is important to note that mortality rates are high in young chickens and can be up to 50%.

Vaccine:

There is a vaccine that can be given. It is important to vaccinate chickens before they are 15 days old. Vaccinating an adult chicken can cause laying to stop.

b) Fowl Pox

Fowl pox, which is also known as chicken pox, avian diphtheria and bird pox is a respiratory disease. It is very common in

chickens and is seen quite frequently in backyard chicken flocks. While they are known as chicken pox, it is important to note that the disease does not cause or is linked to human chicken pox.

Symptoms:

Symptoms are usually very easy to notice, however, it is not uncommon to confuse the symptoms with other conditions. Symptoms include:

- White Spots on Skin

- Decrease in Laying
- Ulcers in the Mouth
- Combs covered in Sores

Cause:

Fowl pox is a viral disease that can affect chickens of any age. It is spread through contact with infected chickens. In addition, it can be spread through contact with contaminated surfaces. Finally, fowl pox has been spread through mosquitoes.

Treatment:

There is no treatment for fowl pox outside of ensuring the chickens are comfortable. Keeping them in warm, dry areas and providing them with food and water will help them overcome the condition.

Chickens that have recovered from fowl pox have a natural immunity to it afterwards.

Vaccine:

Yes, there is a vaccine for this disease.

c) Avian Influenza

Avian influenza, also known as the flu, Avian Flu or Fowl Plaque is a serious respiratory condition that spreads through flocks with a surprising speed. It can be very serious when it affects a flock and it has been known to be zoonotic.

Symptoms:

Symptoms are usually around the respiratory system of the bird and it can be very easy to confuse avian influenza with a more serious condition. Symptoms include:

- Bloody Discharge from the Nasal Cavity
- Red or White Spots on the Legs
- Diarrheal
- Difficulty Breathing
- Wheezing Sounds
- Loss of Appetite
- Sneezing
- Drop in Egg Production

Cause:

Avian Influenza is spread easily through touch and can spread through a flock with surprising speed. It is highly infectious and can be spread from bird to bird or can be spread from contaminated surfaces, clothing or even on shoes.

Treatment:

Antibiotics are usually given to the affected animals, however, it is not always given. Proper hydration as well as proper husbandry will often help the chickens while they are recovering.

Vaccine:

Vaccines are available for this illness, however, they are not readily given and most countries require special licences to vaccinate a backyard chicken from Avian Influenza. It is very important to make sure that you take your own safety into consideration when you are dealing with this illness since it is zoonotic in nature.

d) Infectious Coryza

Also known as a cold or croup, infectious coryza is a respiratory disease. It is very common in illness in chickens, including the

Silkie chicken; however, it can usually be treated without too much difficulty. It does have a low mortality rate, however, the morbidity rate is very high.

Symptoms:

Symptoms are usually around the respiratory system of the bird and it can be very easy to confuse infectious coryza with a more serious condition. Symptoms include:

- Discharge from the Nasal Cavity
- Discharge from the Eyes
- Foul Smell on the Chicken
- Diarrheal
- Difficulty Breathing
- Wheezing Sounds
- Loss in Condition
- Sneezing
- Drop in Egg Production

Cause:

Infectious Coryza is caused by a bacterium that is spread from chicken to chicken through nasal secretions. The bacteria are called the Haemophilus paragallinarum and it is a bacterium that has a long lifespan, able to survive outside a host for 2 to 3 days. It is commonly seen in multi-age chicken farms.

Treatment:

Treatment is done with antibacterial medications, usually administered through the drinking water.

Vaccine:

Vaccines are available for this illness, however, it is only recommend for use when there is a high incidence of the condition.

e) Mycoplasma Gallisepticu

Also known as chronic respiratory disease, mycoplasma gallisepticum is a disease that can affect chickens, turkeys and ducks. It is a condition that attacks the respiratory system and can be very serious.

Symptoms:

Symptoms are usually very apparent when the disease occurs in young chickens and chicks, however, there may not be any symptoms in adult chickens. When there are symptoms, you may see:

- Swollen Sinuses
- Discharge from the Nasal Cavity
- Sneezing
- Foamy Discharge in the Eyes

Cause:

The cause of mycoplasma gallisepticum is from a viral disease. It is spread easily through touch. It is highly infectious and can be spread from bird to bird or can be spread from contaminated surfaces, clothing or even on shoes.

Treatment:

Treatment is usually done through antibiotics. One thing that should be noted is that any chicken that recovers from the disease are lifelong carriers. For that reason, it is important to close off the flock or they will infect healthy chickens you bring in.

Vaccine:

There is a vaccine for this disease, however, it is not always effective.

f) Fowl Cholera

This is a very serious disease that can affect chickens of any age. It often progresses quickly and symptoms are not often seen until a sudden death occurs.

- *Acute:* This is a sudden occurrence of the disease that results in high mortality and morbidity rates. Acute is more commonly seen in young birds.

- *Chronic:* This is a lasting condition that is seen more commonly in older birds. It does not have a high mortality or morbidity rate.

Symptoms:

Symptoms of fowl cholera can differ depending on the type of manifestation. In many cases, there may be no signs of infection until the chicken dies. When there are symptoms, you will see:

- Depression
- Twisting of the Neck
- Mucus Secreted from the Beak
- Infections in the Wattle, Joint, Sinuses or Face
- Cyanosis: This is a dark-purple discoloration found on the skin.

Cause:

The cause of fowl cholera is from a viral disease. It is spread easily through touch. It is highly infectious and can be spread from bird to bird or can be spread from contaminated surfaces, clothing or even on shoes. Finally, it can be spread to other animals on the farm and those animals can infect your chickens.

Treatment:

Treatment is usually done through sulfa drugs or tetracyclines. One thing that should be noted is that any chicken that recovers from the disease are lifelong carriers. For that reason, it is important to close off the flock or they will infect healthy chickens you bring in.

Vaccine:

There is a vaccine for fowl cholera, however, it should never be given to small flocks as it has been linked to a minor fowl cholera infection in some birds. In addition, it should only be given if the disease is in the area.

g) Rickets

Rickets is a nutritional deficiency and it can be caused by not having an imbalance of nutrients. It can also be caused by a lack of vitamin D3, phosphorus or calcium. It is uncommon in flocks where a commercial feed is used, however, it is seen more frequently in flocks where the breeder makes their own feed.

Symptoms:

Symptoms of rickets is more evident in chicks, however, it can be seen in chickens of any age. They include:

- Soft, Rubbery Bones
- Inability to Walk
- Bone Deformities
- Difficulty Breathing
- Soft, Pliable Beaks
- Decreased Growth
- Death

Cause:

The cause of rickets is due to a poor diet. If you make your own feed, it is important to consult a poultry nutritionist to ensure that you meet all the dietary needs of your Silky.

Treatment:

Treatment is done by giving a vitamin D3 supplements and also by improving the diet of your chickens. Finally, offering the chickens limestone and oyster shell is necessary to correct the problem.

Vaccine:

There is no vaccine, however, chickens that are allowed to free range are less likely to develop the condition.

h) Lice

Lice are another common problem in chickens and they can spread through a flock very quickly. Lice are external parasites. They live on the skin of a chicken and feed off of the skin and feathers.

Symptoms:

Lice infestations are very easy to spot in Silkies. The main reason is because you can often see the lice moving through the feathers of the bird. Additional symptoms are:

- Dry Feathers
- Ruffle Feathers
- Nervous Chickens: They will scratch and peck themselves.
- Weight Loss
- Decrease in Laying

Cause:

Lice are a parasite that can be spread from chicken to chicken. Introducing new chickens into your flock can increase the likelihood of a lice infestation, however, they can pick up the parasite from wild birds.

Treatment:

Insecticides that are specifically designed for preventing lice are needed to treat lice.

Vaccine:

There is no vaccine for lice, however, keeping new chickens quarantined before you introduce them to your flock can reduce the risk of developing an infestation.

i) Vitamin A Deficiency

Vitamin A deficiency is a common problem in chickens and it is a result of not receiving the proper nutrients in the chicken's diet. The condition can lead to a number of problems with the mucous-producing glands that are important to the chicken.

Symptoms:

The symptoms of vitamin A deficiency often mimic respiratory diseases so it can be difficult to determine what the problem is. As it becomes more pronounced, it becomes easier to diagnose. Symptoms include:

- Difficulty Breathing
- Difficulty Swallowing
- Crusty discharge around the nostrils and eyelids
- Slow to no growth in chicks
- Depression
- Decrease in Laying
- Death

Cause:

The cause of vitamin A deficiency is due to a poor diet. If you make your own feed, it is important to consult a poultry nutritionist to ensure that you meet all the dietary needs of your Silky.

Treatment:

Treatment is done by giving a vitamin A supplement and also by improving the diet of your chickens.

Vaccine:

There is no vaccine, however, chickens that are allowed to free range are less likely to develop the condition.

j) Pecking and Cannibalism

While this is not a disease, it can be a common occurrence amongst chickens. Chickens naturally peck and you should see the behaviour in your Silky. In fact, chickens will usually peck anything they are interested in and that can include other chickens.

Although the occasional pecking behaviour towards other chickens is fine, when it draws blood on a regular basis, you know that there is a problem.

Often, this behaviour can lead to cannibalism, especially if the chicken draws blood every time pecking occurs.

Symptoms:

The symptoms of pecking and cannibalism can be very difficult to identify since pecking is so normal in chickens. The best thing to do is to watch your Silky flock for signs that the pecking and cannibalism is occurring.

This is usually seen in several ways including pecking at maturing feathers, toe picking in chicks and pecking at the head and vent of other chickens.

While it may start with one or two chickens, pecking and cannibalism is a habit that can be picked up by an entire flock so it is important to combat it as soon as you see it.

Cause:

The cause of pecking and cannibalism can be due to a number of factors and these are:

1. *Lack of adequate space.* When chickens don't have enough space, they will begin to peck to acquire the most space.

2. *Lack of food and water.* Silkies that do not have the proper amounts of food and water will peck so it is important to help minimize the amount of competition between the chickens.

3. *Disease in the flock.* Chickens that are weak or sick are often pecked and it can create a cannibalism problem. It is important to remove sick or injured chickens from your flock until they are well again.

4. *Fluctuation in your flock.* What this refers to is norm of your chickens. If there are chickens that deviate from the norm, it is very common for the other chickens to peck the odd chicken out. This can result in cannibalism. To prevent this, keep chickens of the same breed, size, age and health.

5. *External parasites.* Finally, external parasites can be the reason for pecking to begin. Always check over your flock when you see pecking to rule out all the reasons.

Treatment:

Treatment is not something that can be done. The best way is to provide adequate food and space for your chickens. Keep sick or weak chickens away from the main flock and keep flocks the same. If those methods don't work, you can clip the upper beak to deter pecking.

Vaccine:

There is no vaccine for this condition. Prevention is the best method of combating it.

k) Coccidiosis

Coccidiosis is a condition caused by the parasite Eimeria. It can be fatal in chickens if it is left untreated and there are actually five different eimeria parasites that a Silky can pick up. When the parasite enters the body, it attacks the intestines of the healthy chicken.

Symptoms:

Symptoms are usually overlooked early on in the infestation, however, as the infestation becomes more pronounced, you will see:

- Loss of Pigmentation in the Skin
- Rapid Weight Loss
- Diarrheal

If it is not treated properly and in a timely manner, it can result in the death of your Silky.

Cause:

The parasite that causes the condition is spread from one infected bird to another through the faeces. Eggs are secreted from the infected animal when it defecates. The eggs then stay in the soil until they are ingested by a healthy chicken.

Treatment:

Treatment is usually a water administered medication such as sulfa or amprolium.

Vaccine:

There is no vaccine for coccidiosis. Prevention is difficult as the eggs can be in the soil. Rotating pen location and switching topsoil yearly can help reduce the risk.

l) Capillariasis

Also known as hairworm, capillariasis is an infestation of a thread-like worm. This parasite attacks the crop, oesophagus and intestines of chickens and it burrows into the lining of those organs.

Symptoms:

Symptoms are usually overlooked early on in the infestation, however, as the infestation becomes more pronounced, you will see:

- Paleness
- Rapid Weight Loss
- Diarrheal

If it is not treated properly and in a timely manner, it can result in the death of your Silky.

Cause:

The hairworm that causes the condition is spread from one infected bird to another through the faeces. Eggs are secreted from the infected animal when it defecates. The eggs then stay in the soil until they are ingested by a healthy chicken.

Treatment:

Treatment for capillariasis can be difficult because of the areas that the parasite attacks. The main treatment is Hygromycin B in large dosages.

Vaccine:

There is no vaccine for capillariasis. Prevention is difficult as the eggs can be in the soil. Rotating pen location and switching topsoil yearly can help reduce the risk.

m) Colibacillosis

Colibacillosis is a disease that is caused by E.coli, which is a natural part of the human body. When the disease occurs in Silky chickens, it can lead to a severe infection that can affect the long term health and laying of your chicken.

Symptoms:

Symptoms vary depending on whether the infection is serious or minor. Symptoms that you commonly seen with a colibacillosis infection are:

- Ruffled Feathers
- Coughing
- Listlessness
- Difficulty Breathing

- Diarrheal
- Navel Infections in newly hatched chicks

In addition to those symptoms, colibacillosis can also lead to secondary infections, usually respiratory illnesses.

Cause:

As I have mentioned, the cause of colibacillosis is due to the E.coli bacteria. It is often spread through a flock through the dust and faeces of the other chickens. Chickens that live in dirty conditions are more likely to contract the disease.

Treatment:

Treatment is usually done by antibiotics. In addition, tetracyclines and sulfa drugs may be administered to the chickens and the medications are usually taken for 5 days. One important step to treatment is to clean the facility and to also quarantine the sick Silkies to prevent the spread of the E. coli.

Vaccine:

There is no vaccine for this condition, however, it can be prevented by removing faeces from the coup and keeping dust to a minimum. Finally, never hatch dirty eggs.

n) Ascaridiasis

More commonly seen in turkeys, ascaridiasis is seen in chickens so it is important to be aware of it. It is a condition caused by mold that attacks the brain of the chicken. The condition can be found in two different varieties. These are:

- *Acute:* This is a sudden occurrence of the disease that results in high mortality and morbidity rates. Acute is more commonly seen in young birds.

- *Chronic:* This is a lasting condition that is seen more commonly in older birds. It does not have a high mortality or morbidity rate.

This condition is more commonly seen in males than it is in females, although it can affect both.

Symptoms:

Symptoms for ascaridiasis differ depending on the form of ascaridiasis that your Silkie develops. The acute form, which is seen primarily in young chickens, has the following symptoms:

- Convulsions
- Gasping
- Loss of Appetite
- Sleepiness
- Paralysis
- Death

With the chronic form, the symptoms are:

- Loss of Appetite
- Coughing
- Rapid Weight Loss

- Gasping

Although many of the symptoms are similar between chronic and acute, the chronic form has a lower mortality rate.

Cause:

The condition is caused by a mold that is found in many farms called Aspergillus fumigatus. This fungus can be found in litter, and in the wood of your coop. It can also be found on surfaces that the Silky chickens come into contact with. The mold is even found in feed.

One thing that should be noted with this disease is that it is not contagious.

Treatment:

There is no treatment for this condition, however, it can be prevented by proper husbandry and keeping feed clean and dry.

Vaccine:

There is no vaccine for this condition.

o) Marek's Disease

Marek's disease is a viral infection that can affect chicken of any age. It is important to note that this disease only affects chickens and does not affect any other poultry. The disease attacks the white blood cells in body and causes the bird to develop cancer.

Symptoms:

Symptoms of Marek's disease can vary depending on the progression of the disease, however, it does affect the nerves so you can see many symptoms associated with the nervous system. Symptoms you may see are:

- Difficulty Breathing
- Diarrheal
- Weight Loss
- Paralysis
- Shaking

While those are outward symptoms, tumours are also very common in chickens and they can grow anywhere in the body.

Cause:

The cause of Marek's disease is due to a virus. The virus spreads through the dander and dust of infected chickens to healthy chickens. It can also be spread on equipment and can be transferred on the breeders clothing. The virus that causes Marek's disease has a long life and can stay on a surface for a significant amount of time.

Treatment:

There is no treatment for the condition. All that can be done is to keep the Silkie comfortable. Once the condition has developed to the point that the chicken is in constant pain, it is best to cull the chicken.

Vaccine:

There is a vaccine for Marek's disease and most hatcheries will vaccinate their chicks for the disease before selling. However, the vaccine is not as effective as it once was as the virus has mutated slightly.

p) Leukosis

Leukosis is chronic disease that can affect an entire flock of chickens and it is very serious. Mortality rate for leukosis is at

100% and it is often better to cull the flock instead of subjecting the chickens to suffering.

With this viral disease, the chicken will begin to produce tumours and cancers in its organs. Generally, when one chicken in a flock develops leukosis, about 20% of the flock will develop the condition.

Symptoms:

There are usually no symptoms with leukosis. The bird may show some distress and pain, especially as the disease progresses, however, usually chickens will die without any symptoms.

The disease itself causes tumours and cancers on the liver, spleen, ovaries and lungs. They affect the white cells in the body and often the tumours and lumps are not seen until after death and an autopsy is done.

Despite the lack of symptoms, some chickens will show signs such as:

- Decrease in Laying
- Loss of Appetite
- Diarrheal
- Weight loss

Cause:

The condition is caused by a virus and is usually transmitted through the egg from the environment or the breeder. It can also be transmitted between infected chickens. Efforts are being done to try to eliminate the virus.

Treatment:

There is no treatment for the condition. All that can be done is to keep the Silkie comfortable. Once the condition has developed to the point that the chicken is in constant pain, it is best to cull the chicken.

Vaccine:

There is no vaccine for leukosis.

q) Botulism

Botulism is a condition that affects all domesticated birds including chickens, ducks and turkey. It has also been seen in other waterfowl and in mammals.

It is a serious condition with a high mortality rate, however, the morbidity is low.

Symptoms:

When symptoms occur, they can progress very quickly and an animal can be dead within a few hours of the first symptom. Symptoms of botulism are:

- Tremors
- Difficulty Breathing
- Weakness in Feathers: They can be pulled out easily.
- Paralysis throughout the body
- Death

Cause:

Botulism is caused by the bacteria Clostridium botulinum types A and C, however, other types can cause the condition. It is usually transmitted to the animal through bacterial by-products or drinking water that is infected with the bacteria. It can also be found in some feeds.

Treatment:

Treatment of botulism is done with an antitoxin medication. For early treatment, you can use 1 teaspoon of Epsom salts in 1 ounce of warm water. It should be dripped into the crop 2 to 5 times per day until the symptoms are gone.

Vaccine:

There is no vaccine for botulism. It is important to find the source of the disease and remove it from the area.

r) Moniliasis

Moniliasis, also known as thrush, is a fungal infection that affects the alimentary tract of the chickens, which is the tubular passage for mucus membrane that stretches from the mouth to the anus. It can affect several areas of the Silkies body including the intestine, cloaca and gizzard.

While it is a serious disease, the morbidity and mortality rates for moniliasis is extremely low.

Symptoms:

Symptoms can vary depending on the area that is affected by the condition, however, you will usually see the following symptoms in Silky chickens affected by the disease:

- White, cheesy substance in the crop
- Increased Appetite
- Vent are has a white, crusty substance on it
- Decrease in Laying
- Ruffled Feathers
- Inflamed Vent area
- Droopy Looking

Cause:

Moniliasis is caused by the candida yeast and is usually caused by contact to mouldy feed and water. In addition, it can occur due to poor husbandry and the Silkie living in dirty, contaminated areas. Finally, moniliasis can occur after a treatment of antibiotics.

Treatment:

Treatment is usually done with an antifungal medication; usually Nystatin. It is also important to clean the area and water containers and to remove any mouldy feed.

Vaccine:

No, there is no vaccine for moniliasis; however, keeping the housing of the Silky clean as well as not feeding mouldy feed can reduce the risk of the condition developing.

s) Newcastle Disease

Newcastle Disease, which is also known as Paramyxovirus, is an extremely contagious disease that can affect not only Silkie chickens but any other types of poultry you own. This can include turkeys, ducks and pigeons.

The condition is caused by a virus that is known as Paramyxovirus PMV-1. It can be transferred to other animals and to humans. There are actually four different manifestations of Newcastle Disease in Silkies and other chicken breeds and these are:

- *ND-Velogenic Viscerotropic:* This strain is often referred to as Asiatic or Exotic Bird Flu, it is seen primarily in chickens.

- *ND-Mesogenic:* This strain is commonly seen in older chickens and is associated with nervous system symptoms. There is a high mortality rate with this strain.

- *ND- Neurotropic Velogenic:* One of the highest morality rates when dealing with Newcastle Disease, the viral infection is very acute and leads to a neurological and respiratory symptoms.

- *ND-Lentogenic:* This strain can affect chickens of any age, however, it is considered the weakest strain and chickens often experience mild symptoms with it.

Symptoms:

As you know, Newcastle Disease is a very serious disease and it affects chicks and chickens alike. However, some strains will not see all of the symptoms that I have listed below so it is important to seek treatment if you suspect that your Silky has the condition. Symptoms that you can see are:

- Wheezing
- Cloudy Eyes
- Paralysis in the Legs and Wings
- Twisted Necks
- Nasal Discharge

- Stop in Laying
- Breathing Difficulty

Cause:

As I have mentioned, Newcastle Disease is a viral disease caused by the virus Paramyxovirus PMV-1. It is spread through contact between healthy and infected chickens. In addition, it can be contracted from wild birds that are carrying the virus.

Finally, this highly contagious disease can be carried on clothing, shoes and on any surface the chicken comes into contact with.

Treatment:

There is no known treatment for Newcastle Disease. Some birds will recover from the disease on their own. Once recovered, the Silkies will not become carriers of the disease.

The morality rate of Newcastle Disease can vary depending on the age of the Silkie and the strain of the virus. Young birds under 6 months of age usually have a 100% morality rate.

Vaccine:

There is a vaccine for Newcastle Disease, however, some chickens will need to be revaccinated. They can still develop the condition if they are exposed to a strain they have not been vaccinated against.

t) Omphalitis

Also known as navel yolk sac infection, navel ill, or mushy chick, omphalitis is a hatchery born disease that affects only chicks. It is a bacterial infection and is a very serious condition that can result in the mortality of the chick.

Symptoms:

Omphalitis only affects chicks and is not seen in chickens. It usually affects newly hatched chicks within 24 hours after hatching, however, mortality usually occurs by 5 to 7 days. Symptoms that you will see with a chick that has omphalitis are:

- Weakness: One of the first symptoms is the chicks inability to hold its head up.
- Inflamed Naval Area
- Drowsiness
- Enlarged body at hatching
- Bad Smell to them
- Mushy feeling when you touch them

Cause:

Omphalitis occurs when a bacteria is able to enter the naval of a newly hatched chick. It is more commonly seen in chicks with a weakened immune system.

The main reason for omphalitis is due to chicks being hatched in unclean and contaminated areas. It can spread quickly between chicks in a hatchery.

Treatment:

Treatment is necessary for omphalitis and it is important to treat the chicks quickly to avoid mortality. Chicks should be treated with antibiotics. In addition, any healthy chicks in the group should be housed in separate, clean areas.

The infected chicks should also be housed in a clean area away from other chicks and chickens. The area that the chicks were in should be cleaned and sterilized to kill the bacteria. It is important to note that even with treatment, mortality rate for chicks with omphalitis is 5 to 10%.

Vaccine:

There is no vaccine for this condition. One word of caution with this condition is to handle the chicks with care. The bacterium that causes omphalitis can be transferred to people.

u) Pullorum

Pullorum is a very serious disease where the chickens will develop diarrheal. The condition is very serious and can be deadly for a chicken. It usually affects chicks, however, it can affect older birds.

Symptoms:

Symptoms of pullorum in your Silky chicken can be different depending on the age of the chicken. In young chickens and chicks, you will see the following symptoms:

- Sticky, White Diarrheal
- Inactivity
- Difficulty Breathing

It is important to note that some chicks will die without any symptoms.

In older birds, you may see:

- Coughing
- Poor Laying
- Sneezing

Cause:

The cause of pullorum is from a viral disease. It is spread easily through touch. It is highly infectious and can be spread from bird to bird or can be spread from contaminated surfaces, clothing or even on shoes.

Treatment:

Unfortunately there is no treatment for this disease. All the birds that have been infected by this disease must be culled from the flock. Do not try to cure the Silky. Chickens that recover are carriers and will only create a reoccurrence of the disease in your healthy Silkies.

Vaccine:

There is no vaccine available to prevent this condition. However, a blood test can be done and it is recommended when you purchase any Silkie from an outside breeder.

4. When to Seek Veterinarian Care

One question that many new Silkie chicken owners ask me is what type of veterinarian care their chicken needs. This actually differs depending on the type of animal your Silkie is. If it is a farmyard chicken, then much of the day to day care is done by the breeder, including vaccinating a flock. However, if it is a pet, you will want to pursue more care for your pet through veterinarian care.

In general, chickens don't need a lot of visits to the veterinarian. That being said, it is important to be aware of signs of disease that are common in Silkies, which I have gone over earlier in this chapter. As soon as you see symptoms of an illness, it is important to seek the help of your veterinarian. Most illnesses that target Silkie chickens are very fast working diseases and early detection and treatment can be the deciding factor between the recovery of your chicken or the disease spreading through your flock.

5. Vaccinations

Throughout this chapter, I have gone over several different vaccinations that you can administer to your Silky, however, it is important to realize that you do not have to vaccinate your chicken.

In fact, many people opt out of vaccinating their Silkies for several reasons, the main one is simply due to creating an organic farm. Even big chicken hatcheries will avoid vaccinating for some diseases and it is important to follow some general rules with vaccinating. These are:

1. *Are the diseases prevalent in your area?* There are a lot of diseases out there and some of them haven't been seen in some areas for decades. For that reason, you do not have to vaccinate for those diseases. Find out from local chicken farmers what diseases have been prevalent in your area before you choose the vaccines for your Silky chicken.

2. *Is the flock closed?* What this means is are you adding new Silkies to your flock or will it just be the birds you have? A closed flock doesn't need as many vaccinations

as an open flock where you will be adding new chickens on a regular basis.

3. ***Will you be taking your birds to shows?*** If the answer is yes, then it is important to vaccinate your Silky. The main reason for this is because when a large group of chickens are placed in the same area, it can increase the chance of disease.

4. ***Are you purchasing from other breeders?*** This goes back to having a closed flock but if you are purchasing other chickens from other hatcheries, bird auctions or other breeders, it is imperative that you vaccinate your Silkies. While I recommend that you only purchase from breeders who vaccinate or follow safety standards with their Silky chickens, you can add extra protection by having your own Silky vaccinated.

5. ***What has your own flock's history been?*** Finally, what type of history have you had with your own flock. If you have had certain diseases in your facility before, it is recommended to vaccinate for that disease if it is possible. If not, you can avoid using that vaccine.

If you decide to vaccinate, there are many different companies that offer the vaccines for sale. In addition, vaccinations are offered by veterinarians, however, the cost does increase in this case.

When you are vaccinating your Silkies, it is important to follow these tips, which will make vaccinating much easier:

1. ***Never vaccinate sick birds.*** While it may be tempting, it does nothing for the bird or the prevention of the disease.

2. ***Store vaccines properly.*** Keep your vaccines away from heat and also from direct sunlight. In addition, go through

the vaccines on a regular basis and safely destroy old and outdated vaccinations. They can deteriorate very quickly and will not be effective if they do.

3. ***Vaccinate chicks after 10 days of age.*** There is only oneexception to this rule and that is Marek's disease, which is done within a day of hatching. However, all other vaccinations should be done after 10 days of age or they will not be as effective.

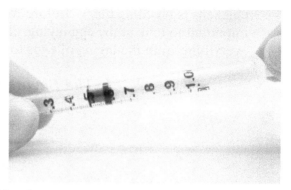

4. ***Choose drinking water vaccines.*** There are several different vaccines that can be administered through drinking water. When you do use the drinking water method, make sure there are no sanitizers or chlorine in the water as those chemicals will kill the vaccine.

5. ***Be safe.*** Finally, make sure that you practice safe habits when you are handling the vaccine. Remember that most vaccines have the live virus in them so if you do not handle them properly, you run the risk of exposing yourself and your flock to the disease. In addition to always washing your hands before and after administering the vaccine, make sure that you burn or disinfect the vaccine containers after use.

And that is all you need to know about vaccinating your Silky chicken and also about maintaining your Silkies health.

Chapter 10. Laying and Breeding

The final topic that we are going to look at in regards to Silkie chickens is breeding them. Before we do, however, it is important to look at the egg laying. This chapter covers everything from the laying of eggs to breeding your Silkies.

1. The Laying Silkie

The very first thing that I would like to cover is the laying Silkie. As you know, many people will purchase chickens for the farm fresh eggs that they can enjoy. However, it is important to note that as egg layers, the Silkie is not the breed of chicken that you should really have in your flock.

Still, Silkies will lay eggs and if you are looking to produce only a small amount of eggs in a week, then the Silky should produce the perfect amount of eggs for your home.

With laying, the number of eggs can be affected by a number of factors in your coop. In this section, I will take you through all those factors so you can be sure to get a good production out of the Silky chickens that you have in your flock.

a) Laying Lifespan

The very first thing that you should be aware of with chickens is the actual lifespan of your hens laying ability. All chickens, regardless of the breed, begin laying around the same age. With Silky chickens, you should see your hens laying between the ages of 18 to 22 weeks. On average, most will begin laying at 20 weeks but some Silkies have begun laying as early as 12 weeks and as late as 30 weeks so don't be too worried if it occurs sooner or later than the average.

When the chicken begins to lay, the amount of laying is actually quite low, however, by 35 weeks of age, the Silkie hen should be at her peak laying age. During this time, laying will be up 90% and you will see an egg on a daily basis.

This peak period usually lasts 8 to 12 weeks, with 10 being the most common duration. After that point, your Silky hen will begin to decrease in egg production.

While some Silkie hens are done laying around the age of 1, many chickens will produce eggs until they are over 3. However, after 3, you may see more complications with egg laying. When your Silky chicken has reached the end of her laying career, she will have laid up to 30 times her body weight in eggs.

b) What Affects Laying

Although we do know that chickens begin laying at a certain age, many people new to Silkies are not aware of the various problems that can occur. When a problem does occur, the Silkie will begin to have a decrease in laying. If you own a Silkie for show, a decrease in laying may not bother you at all but you should keep an eye on your Silky to ensure that there are no underlying health problems.

Reasons that your Silkie chicken may have a decrease in laying are:

1. Light Exposure

Many people do not realize this but chickens require at least 14 hours of sunlight a day to properly lay their eggs. For many farmers, this can be a challenge since local climate can affect the amount of sunlight that the chicken receives every day.

To help your Silky receive the proper amount of light, it is important to use artificial lighting in the chicken coop. It doesn't matter what type of lighting you use but you should make sure that it is bright enough to read a newspaper under. It should not be lighter or darker than that.

Set up a timer for your lights so the Silkies get the 12 to 16 hours of light per day. Most breeders average it out to 14 but you can have a shorter or longer period of light.

2. Disease

The overall health of your Silkie and the flock as a whole, will affect your Silkies laying. There are many diseases that will cause a decrease in laying and that is often one of the first symptoms you will see.

It is important to always monitor the health of your Silkies and all the chickens in your flock. By combating disease early on, you can decrease the likelihood of your chickens have a cessation of laying.

3. Molting

Molting is when a chicken will shed old feathers to make way for new feathers. In addition, during a molt, a hen will rejuvenates her oviduct, which is the organ used in making eggs. It is actually very common and it usually occurs when there is less light in the coop, usually do to winter.

When molting occurs, a laying hen will have a decrease in laying while she is molting. This means that you can expect fewer eggs. Generally, molting occurs at the beginning of winter and you will see more periods of molting the older your Silkie hen is.

To prevent a slow down due to molting, you can prevent molting with the use of the artificial lights. However, you should never stop a molt completely. Inability to molt will result in poor health for your hen and also with a decrease in laying.

The best tip is to allow molting during the winter of your chicken's second year. At that time, turn off the artificial lighting in the coop for 6 weeks. The Silkie will molt and egg production will go back to normal levels after the molt.

4. Nutrition

Proper diet is a very important part of caring for your Silkie and I have discussed it in length in the chapter on feeding, however, I want to mention it briefly now. Silkies that are not given proper nutrition will have a decrease and even a cessation of laying. It is important for both the health and well being of your Silky, and egg laying that you provide a high quality nutrition for your bird.

5. Broodiness

You will often see this with Silkie chickens since they are champion brooders. In fact, Silkies have been known to hatch just about anything and will even wait patiently for eggs to hatch from other species, even if the hatching time is longer than 21 days.

If you are not sure what I mean by broodiness, what I am referring to is the hen's desire to sit and hatch a batch of eggs. This will happen even if the eggs are not fertilized and the main cause of broodiness in a hen is leaving too many eggs in the nest. When this happens, the hen will decide to sit on them and hatch them.

To prevent broodiness, chase the Silkie hen off of the nest when she is brooding, but make sure you only do this if it is necessary. Also, remove any eggs from the nest to help prevent the brooding.

6. Stress

The final thing that I am going to mention is stress. Overheating chickens, moving them frequently, improper handling and not providing them with the proper nutrition can lead to stress in your Silkie. Once there is stress, you will notice a decrease in egg production or a complete cessation of production.

Try to keep your chickens calm to prevent stress. Not only will stress affect your Silkie's egg production but it will affect your Silky chicken's overall health.

2. Breeding your Silkies

Although laying is an important part of owning chickens, everyone who wants to continue their flock will have to spend some time producing young. What this means is that you will have to start breeding your Silkies, however, it is not always as cut and dry as simply placing a rooster with a hen.

a) Choosing your Breeding Silkies

Often, when we look at breeding chickens, we simply choose what we have at hand. Many people who are first getting into Silkies often wind up with both roosters and hens when they purchase a chick.

Because of this, breeding often occurs simply because the rooster has the opportunity to mate with the hens in the flock and you are suddenly collecting chickens. Really, there doesn't have to be a lot of consideration in the rooster and hens, however, it is important to keep the following things in mind:

1. ***Health of the birds:*** The first thing that you should check with your breeding Silkies is their overall health. As you know, there are many diseases that can affect your flock so make sure that your chickens are at optimal health. Breeding sick Silkies can affect the overall health and development of your chicks.

2. ***Size of the Rooster:*** A bigger rooster is a better choice when you are choosing the rooster for your Silkie hens. Bigger birds are often the more dominant birds. In addition, large roosters tend to be healthier than their smaller counterparts.

3. ***Choose by Age:*** While you can breed a Silky as soon as it is old enough to lay, I don't recommend it. Instead,

choose to breed them when they reach their prime for laying, around 35 weeks of age.

4. ***Choose by Colour:*** If you are striving to keep a colour in your flock, it is important to choose hens and roosters that are from that colour type. Don't breed a partridge with a white if you want white chicks and so on.

5. ***Choose by Type:*** Finally, breed the Silkies according to type. Beardeds should be bred to Beardeds, Bantams to Bantams and so on.

When you are choosing your breeding Silkies, it is important to look at the chickens with an eye toward improving your stock. Build on the traits of your chickens and only breed your best Silkie hens with your best Silkie roosters.

After those considerations, there really isn't a lot that you have to consider for your breeding chickens. One thing that should be mentioned is that you don't have to match one rooster with one hen. A rooster can be matched to an entire flock if you desire and it is not uncommon for a rooster to have 3 to 5 hens in his harem.

b) Mating and Brooding

Now that you have the Silkies you want to breed, it is time to start with mating them. With breeding it is important to understand the proper timing. Many breeders will breed chickens all year round or will mate to produce chicks in the spring.

While this practice is sound, I have found that the best time for mating is between February and May. The reason for this is so your Silkies are in their optimal health, which is usually seen during this time.

As soon as your Silky hen has been bred is when you can expect fertilized eggs to be laid. While some hens will lay fertilized eggs for a few days, most will lay them for up to 3 weeks after breeding. Again, it differs depending on the breed and health of your chicken.

With mating, all that needs to be done is placing the Silky rooster in with the Silky hens you are breeding. Allow the animals to become comfortable with each other over the first few days and let nature take its course.

During those days, be sure to provide the proper nutrition for the hens. Hens that have ample access to feed are more accepting of the rooster for mating.

Eventually, the rooster will mate with your Silkie hens by climbing on the back of one. Mating is very quick as the Silkies simply touch their vents together for the sperm to be deposited to the female.

Keep the rooster with the Silkie hens for several days. If you want to produce young year round, you can leave the Silkie rooster with the Silkie hens year round.

As your Silkie hen begins producing fertilized eggs, you will find that she begins to brood on the eggs. What this means is that she will sit on the eggs that she produces and any effort to chase her off the nest becomes difficult.

If you are allowing your Silkie to hatch the eggs herself, allowing brooding is fine. Silkies are champion brooders and they can do extremely well hatching chicks on their own.

3. The Eggs

As I have mentioned, after breeding, your will start seeing fertilized eggs within a day or two after mating. It is important to mention a few facts about fertilized eggs.

1. A fertilized egg will only produce a chick if it is properly incubated. If it is not, it will not produce a chick.

2. Eggs that are fertilized can be eaten. In fact, there is no difference in flavor between a fertilized egg and an unfertilized egg.

3. You cannot open up an egg to see if it is fertile. One myth that seems to abound is that a blood spot in an egg indicates that it was fertile. While this can be the case, blood spots can occur in unfertilized eggs as well.

With the eggs, it is very important that you gather the eggs quickly after fertilization. If you collect the eggs once per day, you should move up your collecting times to two or three times per day. The reason for this is to prevent the eggs from getting dirty, which can lead to disease. In addition, an egg that is not warmed by the hen will be in a state of suspension. The development of the egg does not occur until incubation.

a) Collecting and Storing the Eggs

If your Silkie hen will be hatching the eggs, you will still need to collect the eggs. Don't start brooding before the eggs are ready.

If you are collecting the eggs, handle them with care. Avoid jarring them or banging them together. The main reason for this that you do not want to damage the membrane of the egg. In addition, make sure that you keep the eggs out of direct sunlight as this can cause a number of problems.

Finally, clean your hands before you collect the eggs and keep some wipes handy to wash your hands between nests. Bacteria can be spread from your hands to the eggs and this can lead to health problems in your chicks.

When you have collected them, it is important to wash the eggs. Use a mixture of warm water, no hotter than 35°C (95°F) and an egg wash. Place the eggs carefully into the water, be sure not to bang them, and allow them to sit for 1 minute and no longer than 2 minutes.

Wipe away the dirt with a cotton cloth before placing them into an egg carton with their pointed end facing down in the tray.

One thing that should be noted is that chicken eggs can be stored in an area that is 12 to 15°C (53 to 59°F) for up to 10 days before you begin incubating them. If you are incubating them yourself, you should let them sit in this suspended cycle for 24 hours before incubation starts.

Place the tray onto a wooden board so that one side is raised and the tray is on an angle. Every day, move the board to a different side of the tray so the eggs are angled in a different direction. This is turning the eggs and will keep them viable.

b) Selecting the Right Eggs

After you have collected the eggs, it is important to select the right eggs. Take the time to really look at each egg and look for the following traits:

Dirt:

If you find that an egg is really dirty and has feces on it that cannot be wiped off easily, then you should discard it. There are some diseases that can be spread through the shell and will affect your young chick.

Egg Size:

Choosing egg size is important when you are choosing the eggs you will incubate. The best is to choose average sized eggs. Keep in mind that it should be average for your Silkies since their eggs are slightly smaller than other breeds of chickens.

When you choose eggs, the average sized egg will have the best chance of hatching. Large eggs often have double yolks and small eggs may not have any yolk, which is necessary for the embryo. No yolk, no embryo.

Damage to the Shell:

After you check for dirt and size, take the time to look for any damage to the shell. Even a hairline fracture can lead to bacteria entering the egg. A small amount of bacteria can affect your chick and lead to a number of diseases.

Although some breeders will use nail varnish to repair the damage, I recommend that you do not incubate the egg. While it can be successful, there is still that increased risk.

Abnormal Shape:

Finally, check the eggs for abnormal shape. Not all eggs are perfectly shaped and you can find eggs that are odd shaped, have oblong forms or even ridges on the shell. Discard any abnormal egg and do not hatch it out.

With eggs, it is important to note that only 40 to 80% of the eggs that you incubate will result in a young chick. In addition, the ratio of males and females will usually be about 50:50.

c) Getting a Silkie to Brood

Once your eggs are ready, it is time to get your Silky hen ready. This is done by placing a few fake eggs into a nest for a few days. The hen that will be brooding will begin sitting on the nest and it will be difficult to chase her off of it.

Once you see the brooding behaviour for 24 hours, place the real eggs into the nest. The hen will sit on the eggs for 21 days, turning them as they are needed. One thing that should be stressed is that eggs will not start incubation until they are sat on by the hen.

Many people recommend that you do not get hens to brood since they may not stay on the nest for the full 21 days that it takes an egg to incubate, however, this isn't the case with Silkies.

As I have mentioned throughout this book, Silkies are champion brooders and they are very patient when they are waiting for eggs to hatch. It is very uncommon for a Silkie to not be a brooder so it is usually safe to allow them to incubate your eggs.

d) Artificial Incubation

If you are too nervous with getting your Silkie chicken to incubate the eggs, you can incubate them artificially. This is more time consuming than allowing the Silkie to do it for you. In addition, it can be a more expensive option.

If you are artificially incubating your eggs, you will need the following supplies:

- Incubator
- Anti-bacterial Cleaning Solutions
- Candling Lamp

With the incubator, you want to find one that provides the proper amount of heat and humidity. A good incubator to start with is a Brinsea Mini Eco, which is good for small clutches of eggs.

While you can turn the eggs yourself, it can be time consuming to do so. Instead, choose an incubator that turns the eggs automatically. This will keep you from having to turn them two to three times per day.

When it is time for you to incubate your eggs, it is imperative that you disinfect the incubator, even if it is brand new. This will help prevent the chance of any bacteria being in the incubator.

Once it is clean, do a test run and allow the incubator to run for 4 to 5 hours, or for an entire day, without the eggs. The reason for this is so you can be sure that it is running well. The last thing you want is to place the eggs into the incubator and have it die as you will lose your chicks.

When it has been tested, allow it to run again for until the heat is at the proper temperature. Read the instructions on the incubator to confirm temperatures. Then bring out your eggs. Do not place them into the incubator right away.

Instead, allow them to warm up to room temperature. While they are warming up, mark them with a pencil. Place an "O" on one side and on the other place an "X". The reason for this is so you can be sure that the eggs are being turned regularly.

When they are ready, place them in the incubator. Make sure the incubator is in an area with a constant temperature as outside temps can affect the temperature of your incubator. Always check your eggs during the incubation process. Do not just leave them for the 21 days.

In addition, never add new eggs to the incubator until after the first batch of eggs hatch out. Also, never incubate different breeds together. The reason for this is simply because it will cause problems. Some breeds take longer to incubate and you want them to hatch at the same time.

When the eggs are incubating, you won't notice anything different. You can candle the eggs to determine what eggs are developing and then throw away any infertile eggs.

On day 18 for most breeds, you will begin to hear a pipping from the egg. This is the chick breaking through the shell. By day 21, the chick should be hatched from the egg and you will have a new hatchling.

4. The Hatchlings

Now that you have hatched out your eggs, you are probably enjoying the sight of cute, little Silkie chicks. This can be an exciting time for you and if you are allowing your Silkie hen to raise the young, then there isn't a lot that you have to do.

Actually, Silkie hens are amazing mothers and they will make sure that the chicks are kept with the proper temperatures and care. All you will need to do is provide them with proper shelter.

In addition, you should make sure that your hatchlings are protected from wild animals and birds such as hawks, magpies and crows. The best way to do that is to provide the hen and chicks with a run that has a wired top so the birds cannot get in.

With the Silkie chicks' care, you can leave the Silkie with them for 4 weeks and then remove the hen from the chicks' area. Never remove the chicks as it can be detrimental to both the hen and the chicks.

At that point, they can be cared for as you would care for all your Silkies. Coop them at night and provide them with plenty of feed and water. At 8 weeks of age, you can transfer them to a larger coop and run.

If you are raising the chicks without the care of the hen, you will need a way to keep the chicks warm. The best is to choose a ceramic heat lamp with a ceramic bulb so they get heat and no light. It is important to never subject new chicks to artificial light as this can lead to feather pecking. Instead, use natural light and darkness.

Fill the area with shavings and then place the lamp at one end of the area. You want the chicks to be able to move out of the light if they get too hot. Chicks are very good at self regulating their temperature.

Finally, apply cardboard or wood to the corners to round it off. It

is not unheard of for chicks to crowd into corners and smother each other. Round corners will prevent this from happening.

When you hear piping from the eggs, turn on your heat lamp so the area has the proper temperature. Generally, you want a temperature under the lamp of 39°C or 102°F.

Once the chicks have hatched, wait a few hours until they are dry. Do not move a wet or damp chick out of the incubator. When they are dry, place them in the area. Make sure that you have a waterer in one corner, away from the heat, so the chicks can get water. To ensure this, dip their beaks into the water to be sure that they are aware of the water.

As your chicks become older, you can begin to cull any chicks that have deformities or health problems. It is important to do this as it will maintain the health of your flock.

While some breeders recommend perches for the chicks, I do not. Silkies are not known for roosting and chicks can be easily injured if they fall from a perch. In addition, perches at too young an age can lead to the chick having a bent breastbone.

And outside of the care I have outlined, there really is not a lot that you need to do for your chicks.

a) Feeding your Hatchlings

With feeding, it is important to provide the right type of food. While you can make your own, I strongly recommend that you choose a commercial grade food. As your chicks grow, you will need to switch their food but generally, you allow them to self regulate the amount of food that they are eating.

In general, you should have constant access to food and water for your chicks. It is also good if you choose a medicated feed for your chicks to help prevent some conditions such as coccidiosis.

With chicks, you should feed in this manner:

Starter Rations: 0 to 6 weeks of age

Starter rations are an excellent food that is commonly used for chicks. There are actually several different types of starter rations with higher and lower levels of protein. With Silkies, you want to choose a protein ratio of about 20% since they are not meat chickens.

Another option with starter rations is to choose one that has medication in it. This will help protect your chicks from a range of illnesses and diseases that can affect them.

Grower Rations: 6 to 14 weeks of age

The next type of feed that you can purchase for your Silkies is grower's rations. Again, these should be purchased in a lower protein level since Silkies are not raised for meat. Instead, choose a grower ration that is about 18% protein.

Finishing Rations: 15 to 22 weeks of age

Also known as developer rations, finishing rations is a feed that has a good level of vitamins and minerals, specifically calcium, that will help initiate laying in your chickens.

You should make sure that it only has a 16% protein ratio as you want your Silkies to gain a good weight but not too much fat.

Treats should be kept to a minimal until your chicks are 22 weeks of age or older.

b) Vaccinating your Hatchlings

While vaccinating is an excellent way to help protect your flock, I am a firm believer that you should never vaccinate if you do not have to. Small backyard flocks do not often need to be vaccinated and if you are choosing to have an organic flock, you won't vaccinate.

That being said, the only time that you would vaccinate your chicks is if there is a prevalence of disease in your flock. In addition, if you know that you will be bringing in new chickens, you may want to vaccinate your chicks.

Most chicks are vaccinated for Marek's Disease but other vaccinations are not always necessary. Speak with chicken breeders in your area to find out what vaccinations you should get.

In addition, make sure that you read the chapter on health to determine the vaccinations that are available.

Chapter 11. Common Terms

Throughout this book, I have used a range of terms to discuss the Silkie and while many of the terms are common, it is important for anyone interested in chickens to have an understanding of the common terms used by those who enjoy their birds.

Bantam: A chicken that measures one-fourth to on-half the size of other chickens. A miniature chicken.

Banty: A word often used to describe a bantam chicken.

Barnyard chicken: A chicken that has a variety of breeds in its pedigree.

Beak: The hard portion of the chicken's mouth.

Beard: Feathers that are found under the beak.

Bedding: Materials that are scattered on the floor of a chicken coop.

Biddy: Another term used to describe a hen.

Billing Out: A term to describe scooping feed onto the floor.

Bleaching: The color of the beak, shanks and vent. Usually referring to the color on a yellow-skinned hen.

Bloom: Peak condition of a bird that is used in show.

Bloom: The protective coating that is seen on a freshly laid egg.

Blowout: Term referring to the damage sustained by the vent due to an oversized egg.

Booted: When a chicken has feathers on the toes and shanks.

Break Up: The action of shooing a hen from a nest to prevent setting.

Breed: Referring to a group of chickens that have the same traits and characteristics, such as the Silkie breed.

Breed: The act of pairing a rooster and hen. Done only when you desire fertilized eggs.

Breeders: People who breed and raise chickens.

Breeders: Chickens that are used for producing fertile eggs.

Breed True: Referring to purebred chicks and the characteristics that resemble the parents.

Broiler: A chicken that is raised for its tender meat; usually a young chicken.

Brood: Referring to a group of chicks.

Brood: The caring of a group of chicks.

Brooder: An artificial environment that simulates the protection and warmth of a hen, used with raising chicks.

Broody: A hen that is sitting on the eggs to hatch them.

Candle: The act of shining a light through an egg to determine the contents.

Cannibalism: The act of consuming the flesh of your own species. Some chickens will develop the habit of eating other chicken's feathers, flesh or eggs.

Cape: Referring to the narrow feathers found between the neck and back of a chicken.

Carrier: Referring to a crate or cage used to transport chickens.

Carrier: Referring to a chicken that transmits disease to other chickens. Usually the chicken appears healthy.

Cecum: Found at the juncture of the small and large intestine, it is a blind pouch similar to the appendix.

Cestode: Another term that refers to tapeworm.

Chalazae: The two white cords found inside an egg. They are attached to the yolk and keep the yolk properly positioned in the egg.

Classification: The act of grouping purebred chickens according to their place of origin.

Clean Legged: When a chicken has no feathers on the shanks.

Clinical: Term to describe when a chicken has signs or symptoms of disease.

Cloaca: A chamber that houses the reproductive and digestive organs.

Clutch: Referring to all the eggs laid by a hen during a laying cycle.

Clutch: Referring to eggs that are hatched together.

Coccidiasis: An infection that is free of symptoms caused by the coccidial protozoa.

Coccidiosis: An infestation of a parasite.

Coccidiostat: A drug used to prevent coccidiosis.

Cock: A term referring to a male chicken.

Cockerel: A term referring to a male chicken that is under the age of 1.

Comb: The fleshy crown that is found on the top of a chicken's head.

Conformation: A term referring to the structure of the chicken's body.

Contagious: When a disease can be easily transmitted between chickens.

Coop: The structure where chickens are housed.

Crest: A puff of feathers found on the top of the head. Only common in some breeds, such as the Silkie.

Crop: The act of trimming a chicken's wattles.

Crop: The pouch found at the base of the neck, which bulges after the chicken has eaten.

Crossbreed: Breeding two different breeds of chicken together.

Cull: Referring to a chicken that does not produce eggs.

Cull: The act of killing a non-productive, sick or inferior chicken.

Dam: Referring to the mother.

Dam Family: Referring to a group of chickens that have the same mother and father.

Debeak: When a portion of the top beak is removed. This is used to prevent self-pecking or cannibalism.

Down: Referring to the soft, fur-like fluff of a newly hatched chick.

Down: The fluffy section of the feather.

Droppings: Referring to the feces of the chicken.

Dub: The act of trimming the comb of the chicken.

Dusting: When chickens kick up the dirt to clean their feathers.

Egg Tooth: A horny cap on the upper beak found on chicks. This tooth is used to break through the shell during hatching.

Embryo: The term referring to a fertilized egg during any stage of development before hatching.

Enteritis: A disease where there is an inflammation of the intestine.

Exhibition Birds: Referring to birds that are bred and raised for their beauty and not for laying eggs or for meat.

Feather Legged: Birds that have feathers on their shanks.

Fecal: Term referring to feces.

Feces: The digestive waste, or poop.

Fertile: Referring to a chicken hat is capable of producing a chick.

Fertilized: Containing sperm.

Finish: Referring to the amount of fat that is found under the skin of a meat chicken.

Flock: A term used to describe a group of birds that live together, also refers to a group of chickens.

Forced-air Incubator: A machine that is used to hatch eggs, there is a fan that circulates warm air around the eggs.

Fowl: A stewing hen.

Fowl: Any species of bird that has been domesticated for food.

Free Range: Chickens that are raised to have free access to a yard or pasture.

Frizzle: A breed of chicken.

Frizzle: Referring to feathers that curl.

Fryer: A chicken that is raised for its tender meat; usually a young chicken.

Gizzard: An organ of a chicken that grinds up the food the chicken eats.

Go Light: A sign that the chicken may have anemia. Refers to

Grade: Sorting eggs according to their quality.

Grit: Sand and small pebbles that are eaten by the chicken; used to fill the gizzard and aid in the grinding of food.

Hackles: The cape feathers of a rooster.

Hatch: Referring to a group of chicks that hatch around the same time.

Hatch: The process of a chick breaking out of its shell.

Hatchability: A term referring to the percentage of eggs that hatch during incubation.

Helminth: A type of worm.

Helminthiasis: An infestation caused by the helminth parasitic worm.

Hen: Term used to describe a mature female chicken.

Hen Feathered: Referring to a rooster that has rounded sex feathers.

Host: The animal where a parasite lives.

Hybrid: The offspring when chickens of different breeds are bred to each other.

Impaction: The blockage of a passage or cavity in the body.

Incubation Period: The period of time it takes for eggs to hatch. With chickens, the laying time is usually 21 days.

Incubator: A machine that is used to hatch eggs.

Intensity of Lay: Referring to the number of eggs a hen will lay during a laying period.

Keel: The breastbone of the chicken.

Leaker: A term used for an egg that is leaking due to a damage shell and membrane.

Litter: Materials that are scattered on the floor of a chicken coop.

Mate: Pairing a rooster with a hen or a group of hens.

Molt: Referring to the shedding of feathers; this occurs yearly in chickens.

Morbidity: A term used to describe the percentage of animals affected by a disease.

Mortality: A term used to describe the percentage of animals killed by a disease.

Muff: The feathers that are found on both sides of the face and under the beak.

Nematode: A roundworm.

Nest: A safe place for the hen to lay her eggs.

Nest: Referring to the act of sitting on a nest or brooding.

Nest Egg: An artificial egg, usually made of wood or plastic, that is placed in a nest. It is used to encourage laying.

Nest Run: Eggs that have not been graded.

Oocyst: The egg of a one celled parasite.

Oviduct: The tube that the egg travels through when it is laid.

Pasting: Loose, sticky feces that stick to the vent area.

Pecking Order: Referring to the social hierarchy of chickens.

Pen: The area outside of a chicken coop.

Pen: Referring to a group of chickens that have been entered into a show together.

Perch: Also known as a roost, it is where chickens sleep at night.

Persistency of Lay: Referring to a hen who is able to lay over a long period of time.

Pickout: Referring to damage of the vent caused by cannibalism.

Pigmentation: The colour found in the shanks, beak and vent.

Pinfeathers: The tips of feathers that are just emerging.

Pip: The hole that is formed on the egg when a chick is ready to hatch.

Plumage: The entire feathers that is found on the chickens.

Poultry: Referring to any bird domesticated for food.

Predator: An animal that hunts another animal.

Pullet: A term used to describe a female chicken that is under the age of 1.

Purebred: A chicken whose parents are the same breed.

Range Fed: Chickens that graze freely.

Ration: The amount of food that is consumed by the chicken in a day.

Roaster: A chicken, usually under a year and weight 4 to 6 pounds, that is suitable for cooking whole.

Roost: Also known as a perch, it is where chickens sleep at night.

Rooster: A male chicken.

Saddle: Referring to the small section of back that is found just before the tail.

Scales: Found on the chicken's shanks and toes, it is the hard, overlapping plates on the skin.

Scratch: When a chicken scrapes its toes and claws on the ground; primarily used to find food.

Scratch: Referring to grain that is fed to chickens.

Set: The caring of a group of eggs so they will hatch.

Setting: Referring to eggs that are hatched together under a hen.

Sexed: Determining the gender of the chicks.

Sex Feather: The tail feather in the chicken. Hens have rounded and Roosters usually have pointed.

Shank: The leg of the chicken, or more specifically, the part between the claw and first joint.

Sickles: Long, curved tail feathers that are seen on some roosters.

Sire: The father of the chicks.

Sire Family: Referring to the same chickens that are the offspring of the same rooster; although the chickens may be full or half siblings.

Smut: When black feathers are found on a bird that should not have black feathers according to its breed.

Spent: Near the end of a hen's laying career, it is used to refer to a chicken that is not laying well.

Spurs: Sharp, pointed protrusions that are found on the shanks of a rooster.

Stag: Refers to a rooster that is on the brink of sexual maturity.

Standard: The term that refers to the description of the breed or the ideal specimen of a certain breed.

Started Pullets: Refers to a young hen that is close to laying age.

Starter: Food for hatched chicks.

Starve Out: Refers to chicks who fail to eat.

Sterile: Unable to reproduce.

Sternum: The keel of the chicken.

Straightbred: A chicken whose parents are the same breed.

Straight Run: Chicks that have not been sexed.

Stub: The soft down that is found on the shank or toe of a clean legged chicken.

Trematode: A parasitic fluke.

Type: Used when referring to the size, shape and breed of a chicken.

Unthrifty: A chicken hat appears unhealthy.

Variety: When a breed is divided into smaller groups according to colour, beard, leg feathering, and comb style.

Vent: The opening of the cloaca.

Wattles: The red or purplish flaps that are found dangling under a chicken's chin.

Whiskers: The feathers that are found on both sides of the face and under the beak.

Zoning Laws: Local laws that regulate the raising of chickens in a location.

Zoonotic: A disease that can be passed from human to animal or from animal to human.

CPSIA information can be obtained
at www.ICGtesting.com
Printed in the USA
BVHW091405141118
533117BV00012B/901/P

9 780992 604806